GEORGE H. MORRIS TEACHES BEGINNERS TO RIDE

BY THE SAME AUTHOR

Hunter Seat Equitation, Revised Edition

GEORGE H. MORRIS TEACHES BEGINNERS TO RIDE

A clinic for instructors, parents, and students

by George H. Morris

Foreword by Gordon Wright

ROBERT HALE · LONDON

First published in Great Britain 1983

ISBN 0 7090 1167 9

Robert Hale Limited
Clerkenwell House
Clerkenwell Green
London EC1R 0HT

Printed in Great Britain by
St Edmundsbury Press, Bury St Edmunds, Suffolk
and bound by Woolnough Bookbinding Ltd

This book is for Gordon Wright,
the best teacher of all.

Contents

Illustrations

27. Mounting correctly.
28. Mounting incorrectly.
29. Don't sit down!
30. Shortening the reins—by sliding.
31. Shortening the reins—by creeping.
32. Dismounting—by sliding off.
33. Dismounting—by stepping off.
34. Dismounting dangerously.
35. Stirrup length check—armpit method.
36. Stirrup length check—too far below anklebone.
37. Stirrup length check—too far above anklebone.
38. Stirrup length check—at the bottom of anklebone.
39. Stirrups too long—too open a knee angle.
40. Stirrups about right—correct knee angulation.
41. Stirrups too short—too closed a knee angle.
42. Adjusting stirrups correctly—keeping foot in stirrup.
43. Adjusting stirrups incorrectly—taking foot out of stirrup.
44. Toe on stirrup—wrong.
45. Stirrup close to "home"—wrong.
46. Ball of foot on stirrup—right.
47. Stirrup iron not perpendicular to girth—wrong.
48. Stirrup iron perpendicular to girth; stirrup leather vertical—right.
49. Legs—correct distribution of contact among thigh, knee, and calf.
50. Legs—incorrect distribution of contact; thigh and knee grip.
51. Legs—incorrect distribution of contact; calf grip.
52. Seat bones—toward the front of the saddle—correct.
53. Seat bones—incorrectly slipping to the rear of the saddle.

Foreword

Books are written for many reasons, and the author, from his experiences, imparts the knowledge that he has acquired in the simplest form so it is easily understandable. What it takes to produce this knowledge are all types of experience and many, many years of hard work.

There are some people who can teach and some who can perform. A precious few, the great ones, like George Morris, can do both—he can teach and he can perform.

To be a good teacher one should be capable of using the two basic systems of teaching—"telling" and "copying." The "telling" system is verbally instructing the student what to do, and the "copying" system is showing the student what is correct so he can copy the teacher. I have found in my many experiences and by observing many teachers of riding, that George Morris is a great artist in his field.

I know that anyone interested in any form of riding, be it eventing, showing, jumping, equitation, or just learning to ride for pleasure, will obtain a tremendous amount of valuable knowledge from just reading this book.

GORDON WRIGHT
Landrum, South Carolina

I
Basic Principles of Teaching Horsemanship

Introduction

Teaching people to ride is a very specific and different ability than the ability to ride a horse yourself. That's where many top riders get confused; they know how to ride but they don't know how to teach other riders of different grades. That's what this teachers' clinic is about: the technique of teaching riding.

I call my system the Morris System. There are, of course, other systems. As a teacher develops, his system evolves with him, and if he's a good teacher, he puts his stamp on his students. The Morris System is what has evolved for me. I've borrowed from various people, added and subtracted, and that's how a system is created.

Communication between teacher and student is essential. One of the principal methods of communication is through questions and answers. When I'm educating a rider, I ask him questions for one reason: I ask him questions to see what he knows. If he is not able to explain a shoulder-in, he doesn't know how to do a shoulder-in. If he can explain how to do a shoulder-in, that's the first step toward being absolutely sure that he knows how to do a shoulder-in. So use your questions as a method of communication.

And, in learning horsemanship, it is equally essential for your students to respect the riding facility where they are, after all, guests. Wherever I go to give clinics, I respect the grounds, the rings, the barns, the horses, the equipment, and I'm only a snooper if I ask permission to be a snooper. If I want to go to your barn and snoop around, I will ask you first if I may. This is the sort of manners you've got to teach. We should teach a beginner riding etiquette, professional etiquette, and horsemanlike etiquette as well as horsemanlike technique.

Grounds

As a teacher, your first consideration is your riding establishment. It doesn't have to be an elaborate compound. It can even be a very well-kept, neat little backyard barn where you have three stalls and a couple of jumps in a field. Gordon Wright once said to me: "If you know what you're doing, all you need is a field and two logs." And I'd rather have a field and two logs and Gordon Wright than a Fancy Hill Farms with nobody. Your riding establishment is very important, but a fancy appearance is not. The knowledge that's behind the grounds, their basic neatness, and the horsemanlike approach in maintenance are what count. It's the facility that gives a client or student his first impression. Is it neat and clean and is it presented as a horseman should present it no matter how small it is? I just have a workmanlike place, but everyone who has ever been there will note that it is kept scrupulously clean, and I'm rigid about that. That's why I have to return home about every week or two when I'm on tour, just to check, to see if it's kept that way all the time.

1. *A first impression.* Standards of a riding facility are usually apparent at first impression.

2. *An orderly beginning.* Order and discipline pave the way, whether it is vanning to a horse show, taking a riding lesson, or caring for one's horse.

Even before gauging a teacher's ability, I assess the quality of his stable management. We have some good teachers who produce poor horsemen. They don't know how to take care of a horse; they don't know basic medication; they don't know basic shoeing; they don't know basic grooming, and they do not care. They may be good riding teachers when they get in the ring, but they're not producing horsemen. The keynote to your teaching thought is to produce an all-around horseman. As the student develops in working on the flat and over jumps, he should develop also in the barn.

3. *Maintenance: paddocks, barn, indoor ring, horse.* The maintenance, cleanliness, and neatness of a facility and the animals it keeps are musts.

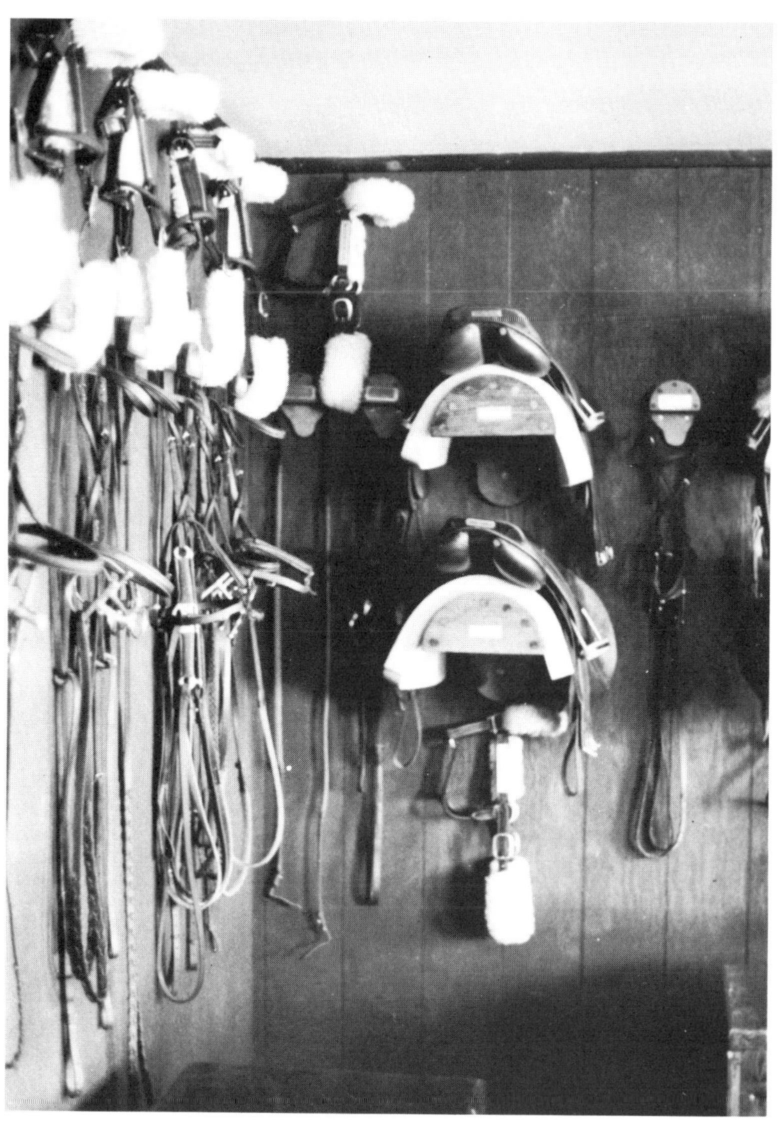

4. *A workmanlike tack room.* Well cared for tack, at the very least, is a safety precaution.

5. *The ring*. The footing of a ring is one's first consideration; the orderly arrangement of jumps, the next.

6. *Grooming*. Good grooming and stable management always precede good riding, teaching, and training.

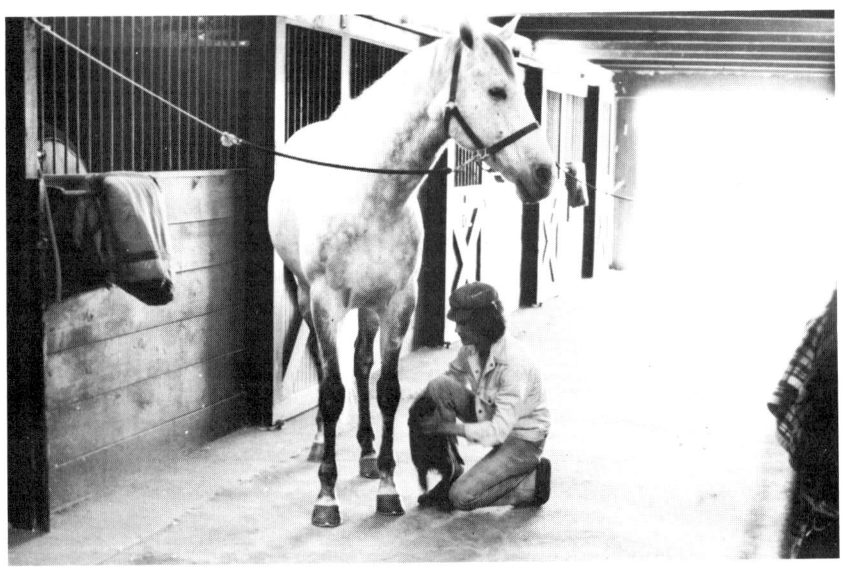

General Conduct

If I had to choose one word that is absolutely basic to my system of teaching, it's discipline. Whether working with a six-year-old child, or a Maclay Cup winner, or a chairman of the board, I require attention and instant obedience. Great teachers such as Bert de Nemethy and Gordon Wright were Army trained, steeped in traditions of discipline. That word, "discipline," is one we're losing in our society. My system demands concentration, and that means discipline.

As soon as a client, a parent, a child drives in, they should be quiet; they should be respectful; they should be polite; they are totally subservient to my rules because I am responsible for their safety, and I am responsible for their progress, and I am responsible for their money in this business. I don't allow

7. *Correct casual riding attire.* While I do not prefer casual attire, it is realistic for our times. At the very least, I expect well-fitting paddock boots, chaps, and hunt caps.

excess noise on my facility, and I don't allow running around. Behavior must be educated and controlled.

As for apparel, I'm very rigid about that, too—both from the point of view of safety, and from the point of view of riding efficiency. There's work apparel and there's riding apparel. I'm satisfied with jodhpur boots and with chaps and coveralls over riding clothes. But I will not allow sneakers or loafers. I think a sneaker or a loafer is, first, dangerous; second, I cannot help to create an educated lower leg if the rider wears a sneaker or a loafer. The rider just won't get the same feel. I don't insist on boots and breeches on a daily basis. Some stables do, and I think that's a little unrealistic. If students are working in the barn and they're wearing coveralls or blue jeans, it takes them two seconds to shift into a

8. *Correct riding attire.* Not only does one ride better in boots and breeches, but it also extends a courtesy to the establishment and the teacher.

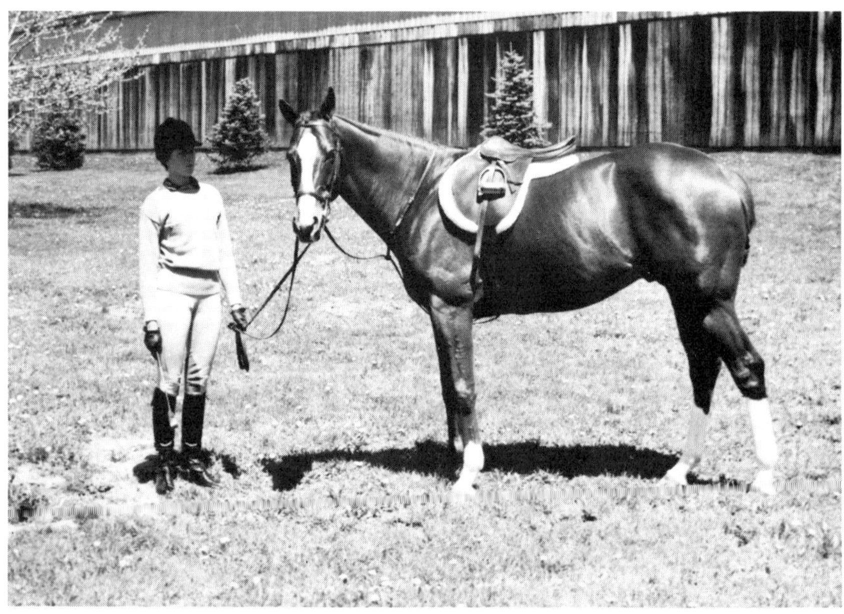

9. *Incorrect riding attire.* Not only does this rider look sloppy, but also from top to bottom she is asking for an accident.

10. *The wrong coat.* Teaching riding is very difficult when the teacher cannot see the outline of the rider's body.

pair of paddock (jodhpur) boots. I don't like those heavy work shoes. I don't allow anything but paddock boots or riding boots. I'm very particular about riders' feet. I'm not sloppy about footwear because the foot is the bottom of the rider's position and structure on the horse. I am very particular about where the stirrup is on the foot and the position of the foot on the horse. So footwear has to be right.

And I won't teach someone wearing a balloony coat. Some of those down coats are passable, and in cooler temperatures you've got to be a little lenient, but I don't like those very thin jackets that billow out. No teacher can see what a rider's doing with his upper body if he's wearing a balloonlike coat. I don't care for riding coats either, in clinics. They're too formal and rigid and unnecessary. A close-fitting sweater—layers of them if necessary for warmth—is best for students to wear.

I'm also particular about a rider's hair. If the rider is coming to the jump, and if her head isn't covered, she's going to be coming to the jump shaking her hair out of the way. I remember a time a year or two ago when I was getting ready for a show in Florida, and I didn't wear a cap. I couldn't school my horses very well over jumps. I was so busy shaking the hair out of my face as I coming to the jumps that my eye was distracted. If head-shaking distracts my eye, it's going to distract a beginner's eye for sure.

I'm very particular about some other kinds of sloppiness too. I don't allow gum chewing when somebody's taking a lesson with me. I chew gum because I talk seven days a week nonstop—much to many people's annoyance—so I chew gum to keep my throat from getting too dry. But riding while chewing gum can be a little dangerous: People have choked on gum—and, besides, it's sloppy. I also don't allow smoking in my classes. When the lesson is finished, they still should not light up a cigarette or chew a piece of gum.

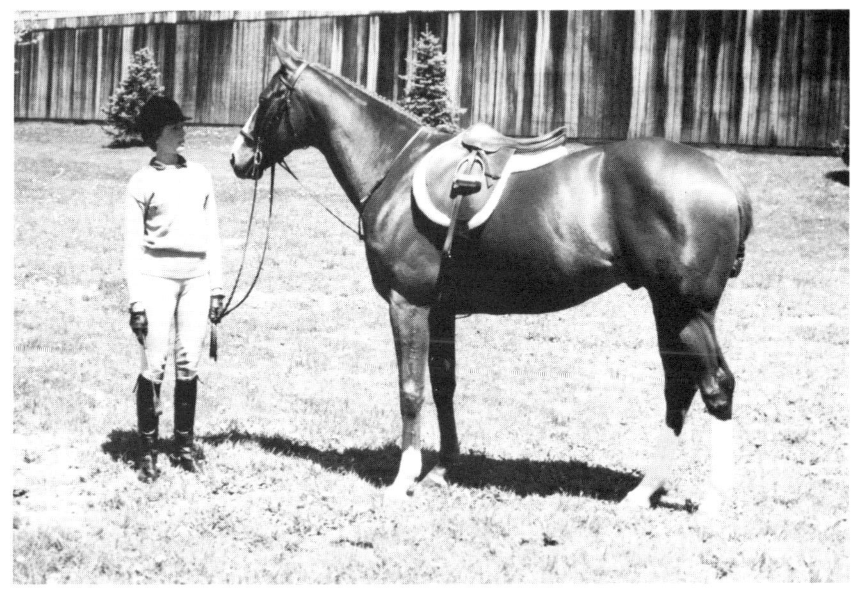

11. *A good sweater and tidy hair*. While this sweater isn't skin-tight, it is form-fitting. Also note that this rider's hair is pulled up neatly under her hunt cap.

12. *Hair!* A preview of coming attractions.

13. *Smoking!* A stupid habit off a horse, smoking while mounted should be forbidden. "Gozzi's" smart eye tells the story in this photo.

14. *Eyes* (*shifty*). A "shifty" eye while riding does not help the steering nor promote concentration.

While I'm teaching I don't allow chatting either. If a couple of mothers chat while watching their little darlings, out they go.

Let's go back to our first word: discipline. I've always stuck to my guns about that, and I haven't lost much business. In fact, I've gained it, because for every student who doesn't want rigid discipline, ten do want discipline. Sometimes somebody will say, "Oh be a little soft with this group." Don't ever soften up on anything. Concentration is not a talent; concentration is a habit. You'll see a rider going around the ring and he'll look out at passersby. When I'm riding a horse on the flat, I don't have time to look out of the ring unless I'm resting or cooling out. I'm bending, I'm regulating the horse, I'm bringing him around, I'm setting him up, I'm backing

15. *Eyes—concentration.* Eyes that work well always bring about concentration. Notice the rider's purposeful expression.

him off, I'm yielding his haunch. With the first-grade pupil, teach the first step of looking at a point ahead, not looking in or out of the ring. Teach concentration.

Authority

The relationships in a riding establishment are important too. In a riding facility there is a hierarchy. There's the owner of the establishment, the teachers, the trainers, the stable manager, the vets, the blacksmiths. To be perfectly frank, the easiest situation is one like mine in which I'm the owner, I'm the teacher, I'm the trainer, and I pay the stable manager. The other setups sometimes aren't as easy, but they work out well if everybody is intelligent and works along together and the right people are in charge.

What I'm getting at here is establishing authority. If the owner of a place is taking a lesson from the teacher, there is just one relationship: teacher and student. If there's a conflict of relationship, then you're asking for poor riding or even an accident. So don't forget the hierarchy of the establishment. Remember that our first consideration is safety; the second is good riding. I can't afford to undermine my reputation as a teacher by risking an accident. Even if you're an old friend, in the ring your relationship with me is that you're the student and I'm the expert and you have to obey me. When it boils right down to it, my reputation as a teacher of safety and riding progress is worth more to me than a friendship.

So you've got to set up the hierarchy in your own facility and make sure everybody co-ordinates well. I leave a great deal of responsibility to my stable manager. I ask for his opinion and usually go with it. I ask my vet and my blacksmith their opinions and usually go along. They are experts in their specialties. Now, when it comes to teaching, they ask my opinion and *always* go with it. A pupil or anyone with a horse in my care has to follow my instruction. An owner can't come running to the in gate and tell me what he thinks I should do going to the second jump. I can't produce that way. No matter how great the animal, I'd say, "Sorry, here's your horse," and I'd find another. As professionals, as teachers, remember that horses and students and owners are basically like streetcars. Some streetcars are more attractive than others or more able than others, but they're still streetcars. You know what streetcars do? One goes down the street, but there's always another one coming along.

My teaching clinics are geared for professionals and for teachers, not for owners, though owners can listen and learn the facts of life. Most teachers, trainers, and professionals lose business from lack of strength, not from too much strength, by catering when they believe something's wrong, by pacifying and saying it's right. It always comes to a dead end. So don't underestimate the importance of relationships in the hierarchy and of being sure orders are obeyed, whether they're to an owner, a groom, or a leadline rider. Such obedience is a crucial safety factor. People in this business tend to underestimate how dangerous the sport of riding is. Jumping is a *terribly* dangerous sport! It is one of the three highest-risk sports. Safety must be your first consideration as a teacher from the beginning to the end. No matter how much money you make or lose, or what ribbon you win or lose, safety must be the prime factor in teaching.

Basic Method: The Exercise System

Everything in my teaching system is an exercise. I see a rider with a poor leg on a horse—it's loose—and I hear the teacher say, "Oh your leg, you've got a loose leg, tighten it." That's not the way to correct a poor leg. What you have to do is say, "You do not have a leg on a horse. Now I'll give you an exercise to give you a leg." We put the leg in position, get him standing in his stirrups for about three minutes a day, and in two or three days he's developing a leg. Maybe in ten days he's got it.

If you want to work on a rider's base of support in his seat, don't give him a seat. The exercise of taking away his stirrups gives him an educated seat.

The exercise system holds true with horses as well as with riders. In the case of a horse that's stiff on the left side of his mouth, his left shoulder and his whole left side are rigid to the left rein and leg. Well, you don't soften him up; the left shoulder-in softens him up. In the case of a horse who is a rusher and a lugger, exercises are to set him on his tail, stop him, back him, set him on his tail. The exercises soften that horse up.

Whatever we do, the sequence is the same: Isolate the problem, select an exercise, and get a result. The result, with both riders and horses, will be commensurate with conformation, talent, and mental attitude. A naturally supple three-year-old tends to be more supple than a ten-year-old that's always been a rigid kind of horse. A rider with only ten hours of experience may be a natural, while some poor soul who's been at it for forty years may be rigid and set in his ways. Well,

God gave one something that He didn't give the other. But you should still improve both horses and riders with a system of teaching by exercises.

Attitudes

A rider's emotions are another very important consideration in teaching riding. There are two types of tensions in a rider: physical fear and mental fear. You have to understand and recognize them in order to teach.

Everybody has some mental fear. When I entered the Olympic arena, I was as nervous as I'd ever been in my life, but I had no physical fear. As you get "longer in the tooth" you develop a bit of physical fear, even if you didn't have it before. I think twice now. But Olympic riders can't have physical fear. I still have a lot of mental fear, but in a show rider, mental fear evaporates when you get in the ring. Physical fear tends to build up in the ring. It helps to know your student. Most beginners have physical fear. Most riders who go into showing overcome physical fear as they get better and better. Nobody gets over mental fear. Some people have more than others, but everybody has some mental fear. With someone who has physical fear, you proceed very slowly. It's best to avoid situations that lead to accidents with someone with physical fear. For one who has mental fear, it doesn't matter as much if he has an accident because the fear is of not doing well enough or making a mistake.

You also have to know about another emotion that's an archenemy to progress and to safety—boredom. We teach by the grade system. A rider's concentration span is likely to correlate with his grade and age. An advanced rider under structured teaching may concentrate for four or five hours. A giddy teen-ager may start out with a concentration span of about ten minutes, but concentration can be developed through formation of good habits. With a very young rider, though—for example, an eight-year-old—never ask for concentration for longer than half an hour or forty-five minutes. After that, you lose their attention. There's no progress, and chances of an accident increase. Sometimes I limit riding time of even those riders with great potential because I want them to want to continue their interest in riding. Otherwise boredom tends to creep in. You have to be alert to signs of boredom as you work with your pupils.

The next area a teacher must be concerned with is confidence. One archenemy to confidence is overmounting. A sixteen-year-old intermediate is overmounted on a hot pony. A tiny little tot is overmounted on a great big horse; he may be a quiet horse, but he's still too big for his rider. Overmounting has to do first with conformation of rider and horse and second with the temperament of each. A teacher must be especially careful about overmounting students on ponies, for ponies are both good and bad as far as overmounting is concerned. I'll have more to say about ponies later. Also, one must be considerate of those who are starting to ride again after a long absence until they get back in the groove. It is difficult for a rider with long legs on a little narrow, weedy horse. Too wide a barrel may be impossible for the short-legged rider.

Overfacing is another crucial tactor in confidence. It doesn't take a big jump to overface many students. Overfacing could be a result of insisting that a low intermediate student get his horse on the bit when the student doesn't yet have the mental concept of how to get the horse on the bit, much less the ability to do it. Or it could be insisting that he do a proper turn on the haunch before he's ready. Many teachers become irritated when students can't do what is requested. But you're asking students to do something in their grade that they're not ready and able to do. If you get irritated, you start a cycle going that becomes trouble. You're overfacing when you ask for results beyond someone's present ability.

It's also important to group students so that the grades are commensurate. The rider who feels outclassed by all the others may get discouraged and convinced that he can never be a good rider.

Qualifications of the Teacher

A teacher should never ask a pupil to do what he, the instructor, cannot himself do or have done at one time. I'd like to see the day when instructors will say, "I'm a first-grade teacher. Now you're ready to go to that fellow in my barn (or another barn) because he's a second-grade teacher." That day's not here yet, because riding instruction is way behind other forms of education. My own temperament isn't suited to taking a lot of babies out on a leadline day after day after day. I shouldn't have that responsibility because I wouldn't be the best one for the job. So we send them to the first-grade teacher and then the second-grade teacher. What I like about this principle is that certain teachers can ask their students to jump a Grand Prix course because *they* can jump a Grand Prix course. I can tell you exactly how to ride that Olympic course because I did it myself. I couldn't do it now, but I have done it.

Most teachers will never be able to take a rider to the level of an Olympic event. They shouldn't expect to, nor develop an ego problem about it. Some won't ever be able to take a rider to the eighth grade because the teacher's niche in life is as a wonderful basic teacher. You might say, "I'm going to learn," and go out and spend money and time. You might learn more and more. But at the very top levels, unless you have done it, you can't teach it. It's a joke to see some of the people in the schooling ring at a Grand Prix. There isn't a prayer that they know anything about what they're telling their riders to do. They're not up to it, and it's really dishonest, not to mention dangerous, to try.

A rider's total belief in an instructor is, of course, another essential. When students doubt me a little, I suggest other teachers they should go to. Without belief, discipline is a mockery, if not downright impossible.

Compatibility of Rider and Horse

Analyzing pupil and horse is, as I've said before, very important. And it brings us now to further discussion of ponies. From a conformation point of view, they're good for a young child. But often, from the point of view of temperament, a pony is not a very good choice because a pony tends to be strong-minded and stubborn. A pony often is a lugger and a grass-eater and a bulger and a tugger. It takes an expert to straighten him out. Ponies often learn to put on the brakes while jumping. Today ponies are bred closer to Thoroughbreds, and these ponies' temperaments are better. But, as a rule, ponies are likely to produce riders who act like cowboys. Gordon Wright never let children ride ponies for that reason. After two or three years you have a habitual rough rider. Then it'll take three or four or ten years or never to make him into a polished rider. I'd rather have a big horse with a good temperament as a school horse than a little pony who's a little bully and stubborn. You can't very often teach a child to ride with finesse that way.

The riding instructor should analyze the pupil and the horse in every lesson situation. Are they compatible in conformation? As for age—well, there's an old adage: young horse, young rider—no good. I tried it, and I learned it's wrong. It just doesn't work. Very often when a poor lower amateur or lower junior rider doesn't have much money to spend, you try to save him a dollar and get a three-year-old, then you're in for a long haul. A young rider doesn't have to be youthful chronologically; he can be a forty-year-old amateur who's got a certain number of hours of training in the saddle. Matching the temperaments of the rider and the horse is certainly as important as achieving congenial conformation. If I have an overriding boy, I get him a horse that's a little sluggish. If I have an underriding, somewhat timid girl, I get her a horse that's a little bold, that will carry her. Everybody's an underrider or an overrider to some degree. Riders can always be categorized by temperament.

You can observe a rider's instinct when he works with a horse and especially when he gets in trouble with one. In fact, you ought to be something of a psychologist as you work with people. With one student you would have to hit her over the head with a two-by-four to get her attention. With another, who is attentive and interested and anxious to learn, if you hit her over the head she'll develop such mental fear that she can't function. For still another, the only way you get her attention is by embarrassing her.

In analyzing riders it is desirable to grade them. Don't

16. *Conformation.* The length of a rider's leg and the size of a horse's barrel determine the compatibility of horse and rider conformation, rather than the height of the horse or the length of the rider. Here is a long leg on a narrow barrel.

17. *Conformation.* Here is a bit of a short leg on a bit of a wide barrel.

18. *Conformation.* Physically these riders fit their horses well.

count how long they've ridden, how many hours they've had in the saddle, but try to grade them according to your technique and your system. How much they know and can do are the keys to which grade they're to be in.

In teaching, I prefer doers to talkers or commentators. (I include teachers in this.) Bragging and predicting success about your horses or pupils is a poor habit. Shut your mouth. Just show what you or they can do.

One Step at a Time

Simplicity is a basic part of my system; we teach one thing at a time. When we teach a rider about his legs, we don't worry about his hands. When we teach a rider about a shoulder-in, we're not too much worried that he's got a little

19. *Magnetism.* A riding teacher must hold his audience's attention, and rarely, if ever, be boring.

roach in his back. If we're teaching a rider about his release at a jump, we're not worried about his eyes. Especially at low levels of riding, we're very strict about keeping things simple.

At first, we teach essentially one thing at a time. Later we teach a sequence of two or three things, step by step, in a row. When a rider knows each of the little parts, then we put them together. When teaching is done this way, learning is quicker. It takes longer to learn if the rider is taken out into the ring without a simple program or structure. He's confused if several instructions are thrown at him at once, over and over again. That's what we call cluttering.

Communication

Questions and answers are one form of communication, as I pointed out at the beginning of the clinic. But now we come to a teaching sequence of four steps in communication: (1) explanation, (2) demonstration, (3) observation, and (4) repetition.

Explanation must be clear, loud, and precise. I've seen teachers who mumble or have other speech problems. They should attend a speech class. Many teachers are not precise. "Well, your shoulder-in, you bend your horse, and you go down the wall, and he's, he's going, I think it's on two tracks he's on, and well, go out and do that, go out and try that." Or, "Gee, there's something about your back over the jump that . . . go do that jump again." In the latter instance, if the rider is ducking his upper body, he has a roach in his back; and in the air he's looking at the jump, which is creating the duck and the roach. The instructor ought to be able to tell the rider *exactly* what he's doing wrong. That's the precision part of teaching. The instructor should be able to give an explanation clearly, loudly, and precisely.

Demonstration is the second form of communication. I grew up with a teacher, Gordon Wright, who is, I think, the greatest I've ever met. He was a born teacher, just a born teacher. He always taught us that we were a step ahead if we could get on a horse and demonstrate. But often many of those who can demonstrate can't explain what they are doing. Actually, all of us should learn how to explain better. My goal is constantly to teach what we've always taught, but to teach it better.

20. *Demonstration from the ground.* Here the teacher is giving a "picture" of correct thumb angulation.

You can demonstrate on the ground—for instance, correct thumb position, or correct head and neck carriage. And you should be able to demonstrate on a horse.

Observation, another must, is the third step. I go to shows to see what others are doing. An instructor ought to take students to shows to observe, watch, and copy the good and leave the bad. Of course, it's an edge for a rider to have a teacher or a trainer who is an artist, because students do copy!

Repetition is the fourth step in the sequence, and it's the best way to develop a habit. It reinforces what they are learning. First, explanation. Students go out and practice (application and correction). Then demonstration. I go out and show them. More practice (application and correction), but what gives them the technique is repetition, over and over and over again. It is called brainwashing.

With these four steps—explanation, demonstration, observation, and repetition—a pattern evolves: the rider's ability to handle variation. I expect a horseman and a pupil to be able to cope with anything. One day we'll ride without stirrups, we'll ride on the flat, we'll ride over gymnastics, we'll ride cross-country. Students will ride green horses, jumpers (if they've graduated to that level), saddle horses, and/or stock horses if there's the opportunity. Variation develops a rider. Give him as much as possible. Even several teachers, each with a different strong point, can provide variation, but different systems going at the same time cause confusion and are not desirable.

A cardinal rule for any teacher is never, never to allow self-satisfaction—in himself or in a pupil. If you see evidences of it, nip it in the bud. I often put smug riders on rough horses (letting the riders have a problem or two), or I ask them to do a zigzag traverse on the flat when they don't know what it is. Immediately they know they're not very good. As for me, I can never get too self-satisfied because I'm always being beaten. I don't win every class. How can you feel self-satisfied when you're being beaten? The idea is to review and review at every level of riding. I have a top rider in a low group. He's reviewing his leg. He's reviewing his release. He's reviewing this and that.

Education for the Teacher

I'm also a great believer in reading. As teachers you should be aware of other methods and other systems. Study other methods and other systems. Take what you like from them. Discard what you don't like. You should try everything.

You especially want to try what the rider who's beating you does—or what his pupils do. I learned something in the old days: If something doesn't work for you, change. A snaffle bit is best for making the horse end up as a Grand Prix dressage horse. It is not the best bit for ending up with the best performance over jumps. Why not? Because you're working with a galloping horse at fast paces, and that is not the same as riding in the dressage square. They're two different disciplines. Many things coincide, but many do not. But I see people with fat snaffles and no martingales hoping, hoping, hoping to get beautiful performances on hunters and jumpers. Year after year they're not getting the desired results. So if something doesn't work, change.

Finally, keep up with the times, keep watching, stay abreast of the others.

Technique and Position

If possible, continue taking lessons. I learned a little thing when I was an actor from a book by the great dramatic teacher Stanislavsky: At first technique is difficult, but as it becomes a habit, it gets easy, very easy; at last it becomes beautiful.

I also learned something from a modern dance genius, Martha Graham: total physical control. Total physical control sets a rider free to ride a horse. That's why I'm a position nut. Some born athletes can probably get away with anything, but we're talking about teaching in riding schools with hundreds, thousands of adults, juniors, beginners, all kinds. I'm a stickler on position because instructors have to work with the average rider, and when the average rider's position is correct

21. *Posture demonstration and application.* Here the "picture" denotes posture, pose, and theatricality. In other words—excellence!

and set according to my ideals, he is then more free to function and to ride his horse correctly.

Group Teaching

In our system, we work a group in three ways. The first is with a fixed distance. Depending on the area, we'll work two horses or three or four or five, each spaced at a definite distance apart. It's an exercise in concentration, an exercise that teaches control.

The second method of working a group is without a fixed distance. Everybody goes to the left, for example, but they're riding on their own, trotting, stopping, backing, circling. Every rider does the same thing and goes the same way at the

22. *Group riding instruction.* A minimum distance for safety is one horse's length apart.

23. *Group riding instruction.* Having ridden in, a slight semicircle is a bit safer than a straight line-up.

same time, but the riders don't necessarily ride one behind the other.

The third method is to have riders working at will—that's only for a good group. I let them go out into the ring and do whatever they want. Then I call them in. I explain and send them all back into the ring to do what they want. Then they stand still and I get on a horse and demonstrate.

The fixed distance gives the teacher one very special advantage. People sometimes wonder at how easily I seem to learn names, even thirty names a day. It's not that I'm brighter than anybody else. It's the trick of the fixed distance: Susie, Mary, Sally; Susie, Mary, Sally, Ann; Susie, Mary, Sally, Ann, David; Susie, Mary, Sally, Ann, David, Ian. Now you understand why I have such a temper fit when anyone gets out of order!

24. *Adjustment of a jointed snaffle—right and wrong.*
Left: The bitting on the horse is too low; there are no wrinkles in the corners of his mouth.
Right: Correct bitting; there are a couple of wrinkles in the corners of his mouth.

II
Teaching the Beginner on the Flat

Tack

First we're going to teach about tack and its adjustment. We'll start with the *jointed bit*. With the jointed bit you will see a couple of wrinkles at the horse's mouth. With a *straight bit* you see only half a wrinkle, not two or three.

Now let's go to the *martingale*. I don't use or advocate a running martingale for young riders, either beginners or intermediates, because it gets them into a whole lot of trouble, acting on the sensitive bars of the horse's mouth. What you want to use with beginners or intermediates is the standing martingale. It should never touch the throat, for that means it's too long. I always advocate using standing martingales with beginners, but when riders develop to intermediate level, I let them work on the flat without a martingale. I always have advanced riders work on the flat without a martingale so they can learn to keep their horses on the bit without that aid.

Next we'll discuss *saddles*. Nowadays we don't like too much depth in saddles, because that separates the rider from his horse. Nor do we want, with a beginner, a totally flat saddle. A Hermes is perhaps too flat a saddle for a beginner. A beginner needs a modified one with a knee roll or two. Make

25. *Standing martingale—a little on the long side.* There is no point to a standing martingale if there is too much play.

26. *Standing martingale—a little on the short side.* This is, as a rule, the lesser of the two evils.

sure that the saddle fits with proper length from the pommel to the cantle and proper length of the stirrup.

Mounting and Dismounting

After your riders are tacked up correctly, you're ready to teach them to mount properly. In teaching to mount, have the student face three quarters to the rear; if the horse walks forward, the rider will catch up with him as he swings up. The second step is to take the reins in the left hand. The outside rein should be a little shorter than the inside rein, so that the horse's haunch goes in a little to the left. If the horse backs up, the rider doesn't prevent him but follows until he stops backing. The left hand grasps the crest of the horse's neck, not the pommel of the saddle. Now the rider puts the left foot in the stirrup with the toe facing the girth. Now he steps on. The right leg swings over, and the right foot gets the other stirrup. When the weight is in the right stirrup, the rider sinks onto the horse's back very gradually and slowly. If you teach your pupils to mount without getting the right stirrup, if you let them drop into their saddles, they find themselves on the ground pretty quick, especially if it's a young, green horse. So teach them from the beginning how to mount the right way because the first riding relationship with a horse is mounting.

Now the rider should take up the reins in both hands and shorten the reins by sliding. Demonstrate the difference between sliding and creeping. You have to teach a rider everything—don't assume that a pupil knows a thing. You shorten reins by sliding, not by creeping. Separate the little finger and the third finger and run the single rein between them. Some good riders have the little finger inside the rein. That's all

27. *Mounting correctly.* Contact with horse's mouth, outside (off) rein a fraction shorter, stick in the left hand, left hand grasping crest of the neck, rider three quarters to the rear of her horse, left toe in the stirrup and the girth.

28. *Mounting incorrectly.* No contact with horse's mouth, horse bent toward rider, rider facing side of horse, horse's haunches moving away, toe in the horse's ribs causing irritation.

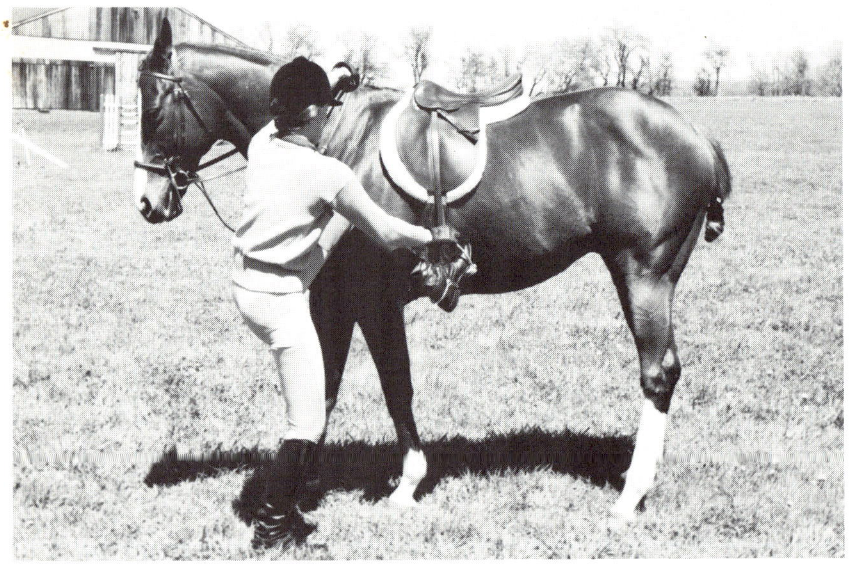

29. *Don't sit down!* Upon mounting, rider picks up off stirrup first; he then gradually sinks into horse's back and adjusts his basic position. One may allow a "fresh" or a "hot" horse to move off at a walk while this is being done.

30. *Shortening the reins—by sliding.* The most economic way to shorten one's reins is to take the *left* rein with the right thumb and index finger and slide up the *left* rein with the left hand. Vice versa for the right rein.

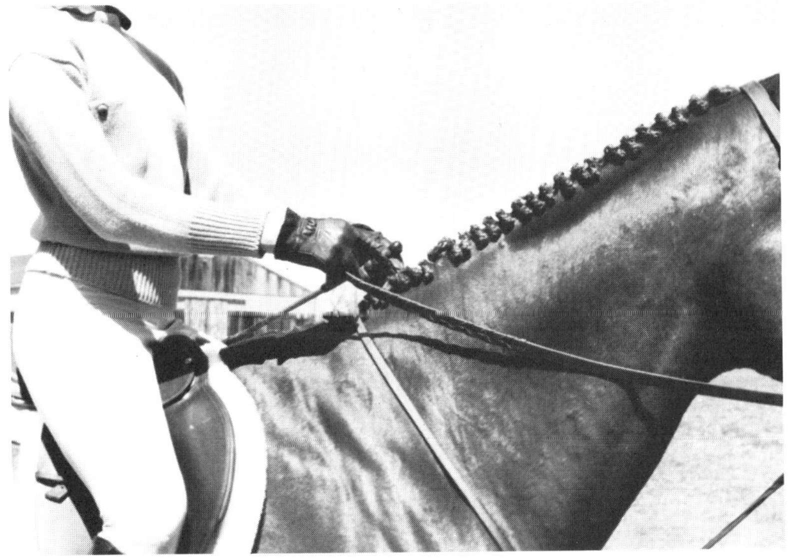

right, but I prefer the little finger outside because it gives a double grip. The thumb is the first grip, and the little finger is the second grip, and these are the grips that prevent your reins from slipping.

Next let's teach dismounting. The two ways of dismounting are to slide off and to step off. To slide off, the rider takes both feet out of the stirrups, swings the right leg behind and over, and literally slides down. Stepping off is perhaps more comfortable for an adult, though sliding off seems safer. In stepping off, the rider takes the right foot out of the stirrup, then swings over, and before the right foot touches ground, releases the left foot and steps down.

31. *Shortening the reins—by creeping.* To open one's fingers and grasp and creep up the reins is slower. This method often produces a dropped rein.

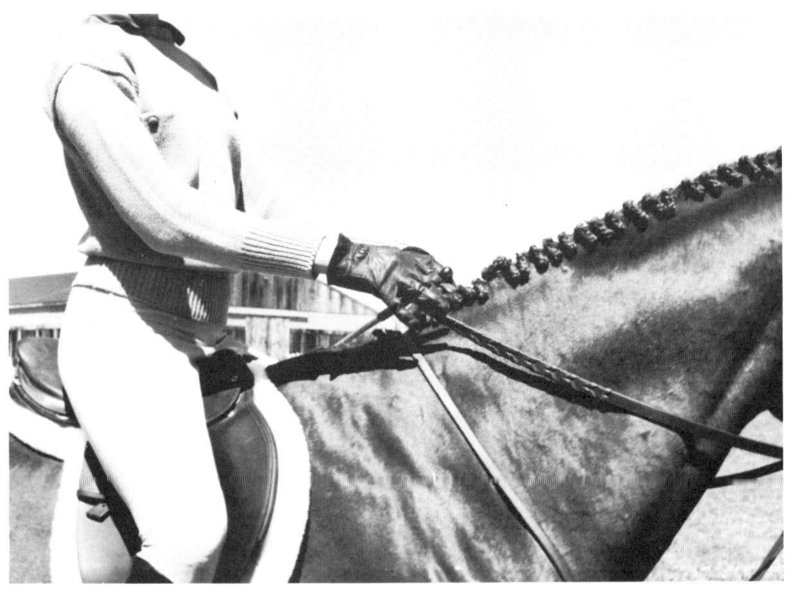

32. *Dismounting—by sliding off*. Contact with horse's mouth, reins in the left hand resting on horse's crest or withers, both feet out of stirrups, rider swings right leg over croup and slides off. (In dismounting, the horse must be made to stand.)

33. *Dismounting—by stepping off*. The only difference in this method is that the rider keeps his left foot in the stirrup until the right foot is parallel to it. I prefer sliding off.

34. *Dismounting dangerously.* The worst fall I've ever had riding a horse resulted from this type of dismount. My spur caught my three-year-old filly's neck, she bolted, and I was thrown under her galloping hind legs.

Stirrup Length

Now check the stirrup length. The first way for an average rider is to use the armpit method. With the hand touching the stirrup bar and the arm extended straight, the stirrup iron should touch the armpit. The second way is, when mounted, to drop the feet out of the stirrups. The stirrup iron should hit at the bottom of the anklebone, just under the anklebone—not an inch under it or on top of it. That's the basic length. For dressage you want to drop the iron, perhaps an inch under the anklebone. If the rider is going over big courses, it might be half an inch above the anklebone. As the jumps get

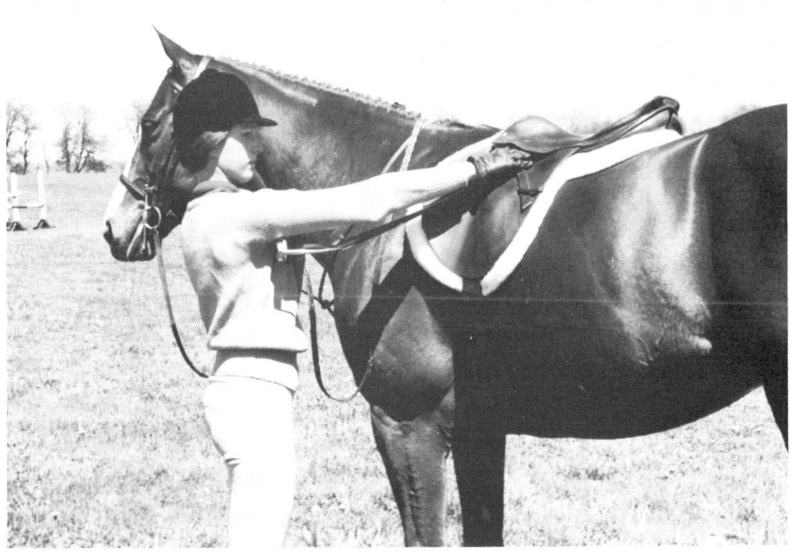

35. *Stirrup length check—armpit method.* The fingertips must touch the bar; the stirrup leather held taut; and the bottom of the stirrup iron fit snugly into the armpit. Your stirrup length should be about right.

36. *Stirrup length check—too far below anklebone.* Gently bounce the foot against the bottom of the stirrup iron. Where does it hit?

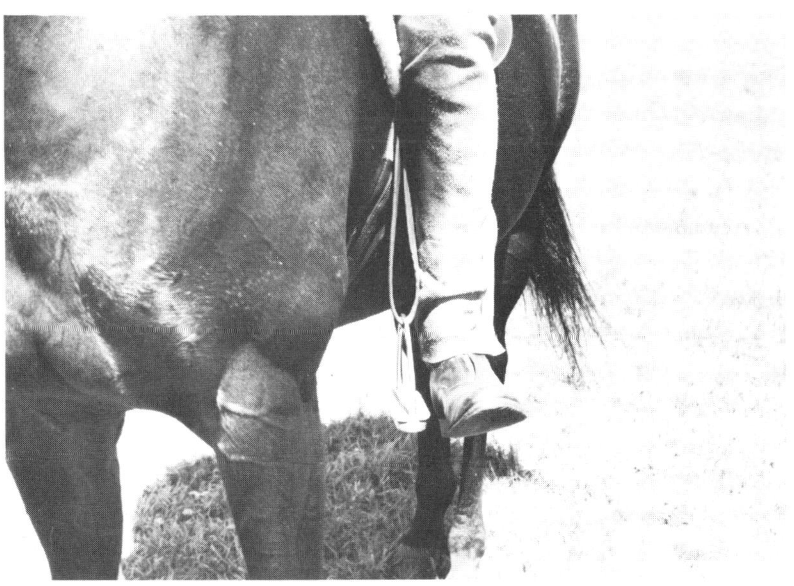

37. *Stirrup length check—too far above anklebone.* The stirrup hits the inside of the rider's shin.

38. *Stirrup length check—at the bottom of anklebone.* For all-purpose riding, this is the ideal length. For more extensive flatwork—a little longer; for more extreme galloping and jumping—definitely a bit shorter.

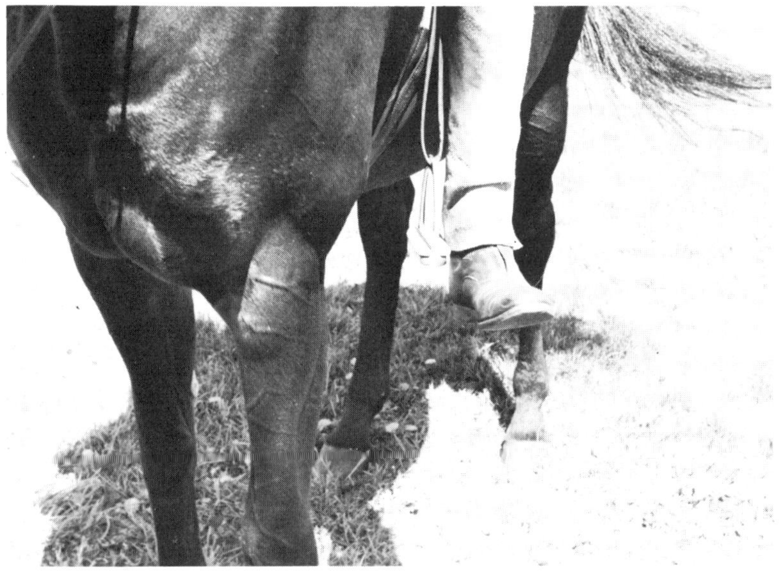

39. *Stirrups too long—too open a knee angle.* The rider appears to be reaching for his stirrups and his knee angle is rather open. This length stirrup does not give enough support for faster work but is right for dressage.

bigger, the stirrups are shortened a little. So there might be a range to cover work on the flat, hunting, jumping, puissance—there might be a four-hole difference depending on the activity. But for the average beginner as well as for the intermediate, there should be just one all-purpose length of stirrup. It should be at the bottom of the anklebone. Don't shift stirrups until a student is pretty good at the intermediate level. Then you can go to two different-length stirrups.

The best check of stirrup length is your instructor's eye. I judge it by the knee angulation—the angle from the rider's thigh to his calf. The instructor should watch, especially at the trot, to see whether the angle is too closed or too open.

The first step in working with riders in a group lesson is to make sure their stirrups are the right length. You can't do anything with the group until their stirrups are the right length.

Now let's tackle how to adjust stirrups when mounted. Most people take their feet out of the stirrups. Suppose I'm on a cold-backed two-year-old and my stirrups are too short and I want to sneak them down a hole or two. If I take my foot out and start adjusting my stirrup, I'll end up on the ground. *No!* Don't let them take their feet out of the stirrups. Have them open their knee and thigh and then adjust the stirrups.

Basic Position at the Standstill

In defining the basic position, we teach in our system that there are four parts to the rider's body. The first part is the lower leg. That's from the knee on down. The second part is his base of support. That is everything touching the saddle, including the seat. The upper body is the third part, and the fourth part is arms and hands. We divide the body like that to simplify and to isolate the parts in order to teach better.

In making adjustments to achieve the basic position, we start with the rider's lower leg, which is his security. In our system the lower leg is the most important part, not the seat. First we check the *stirrup position* on the foot of the rider. The stirrup should be placed on the ball of the foot. Beware of the stirrup out on the toe—there's no support when it's on the toe. And if it's back of the ball of the foot, there's no leverage to get the weight flexed into the heel, which is the anchor on a horse for the average rider. The anchor on an

40. *Stirrups about right—correct knee angulation.* It is up to the teacher's experience and eye to evaluate the rider's knee angle, which should be neither too closed nor too open.

41. *Stirrups too short—too closed a knee angle.* By raising the stirrup, the knee is raised and the buttocks pushed to the back of the saddle.

42. *Adjusting stirrups correctly—keeping foot in stirrup.* For the sake of safety and economy, one should never take the foot out of the stirrup to adjust the stirrups; simply open the knee and thigh.

43. *Adjusting stirrups incorrectly—taking foot out of stirrup.* Not only would this rider be in trouble if the horse bucked or bolted, but when the foot is in the stirrup, it is also much easier to push down on the iron to lengthen and to pull up on the iron to shorten.

44. *Toe on stirrup—wrong.* It is certainly easier to lose a stirrup in this position; also, the support of the rider's weight is minimized.

45. *Stirrup close to "home"—wrong.* Here the stirrup has slipped back, thus preventing elasticity and flexion of the ankles.

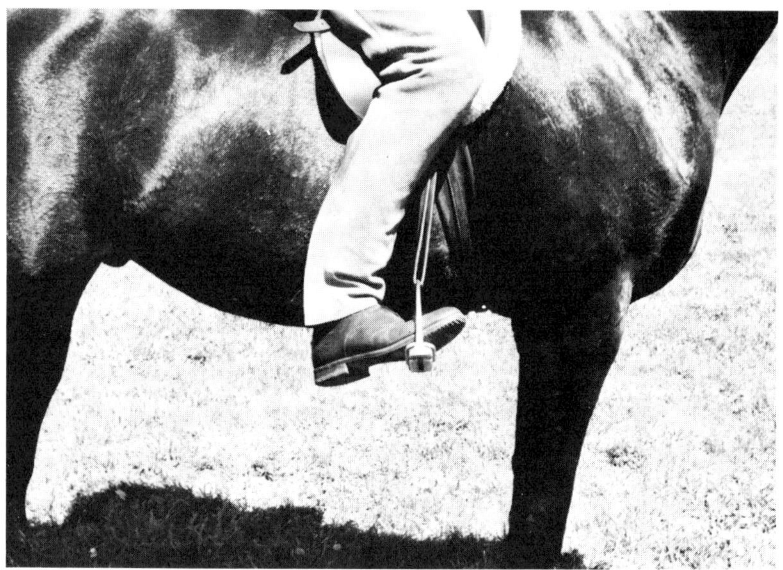

46. *Ball of foot on stirrup—right.* The first step of obtaining this classic leg is by placing the ball of the foot on the middle or outside of the stirrup iron.

47. *Stirrup iron not perpendicular to girth—wrong.* The twist of the outside branch of the stirrup iron to the rear not only looks ugly but also can bring the toes out too far.

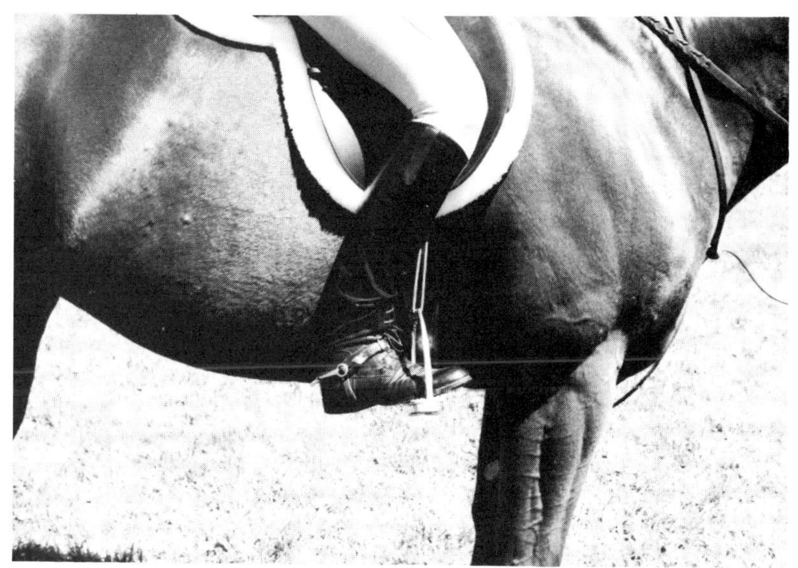

48. *Stirrup iron perpendicular to girth; stirrup leather vertical—right.* This position of the stirrup iron not only looks cleaner but it also helps maintain the toe angulation.

athlete or a genius or a most experienced rider can be standing on the left ear of a horse. But we're not teaching the greats; we're teaching average students.

As to the *twist of the stirrup,* you're going to think I'm a detail nut, and you're right. The twist of the stirrup should be perpendicular to the girth. That is important and I've recently come to feel it is even more important than I used to think. The foot should preferably be on the center or on the outside. If it's on the inside, it often gives the rider a cocked-foot feel. On the center or at the outside rim, it gives a flat feel rather than a cocked feel. The Army used to teach the inside position. You still see it, but it's not as good a foot feeling or as good a leg as having the foot on the flat center or the outside rim of the stirrup.

49. *Legs—correct distribution of contact among thigh, knee, and calf.* The correct leg does not promote an excessive grip; rather, it simply envelops the horse's barrel.

50. *Legs—incorrect distribution of contact; thigh and knee grip.* The rider's calf is helplessly away from the horse. He is pinched up on top of his horse by knees and thighs alone. This is most definitely an old-fashioned way to ride.

With the stirrup iron turned perpendicular to the girth and the weight in the heel, the stirrup leather should hang straight down, not be pulled back or pushed forward.

Now what about *contact distribution?* Contact distribution only in the knee and thigh is outdated and wrong. Contact with only the lower leg is also wrong. It's best to distribute the contact evenly into three places: the thigh, the inner knee bone, and the calf.

Let's consider another part of the body, the *base of support*. The main thing about the base of support is that it should be up in the front of the saddle, not back in the cantle, with the rider sitting on his seat bones. I teach using the buttock and the crotch for certain situations, and we'll get to that later, but the basic position is the seat-bone position.

51. *Legs—incorrect distribution of contact; calf grip.* This grip is even worse as the rider is literally hanging on by the lower legs, which are meant to be sensitive aids.

52. *Seat bones—toward the front of the saddle—correct.* Notice the amount of space between the cantle of the saddle and the rider's buttocks. She is promoting this position by grasping the pommel and pulling herself forward and down into the saddle.

53. *Seat bones—incorrectly slipping to the rear of the saddle.* This is a most faulty position. First, it is most uncomfortable and damaging to the soft loins of the horse's back. Second, it is a more difficult place for the rider to sit comfortably and follow the horse's movement.

At a standstill, the *upper body* is on the vertical—not in front of the vertical or behind the vertical—but *on the vertical,* and in the basic position, with the rider looking up and ahead. The shoulders are relaxed, not tensed, and the back is straight. You don't want a roach back—that's a teacher's term for a round back. And you don't want an overly arched or sway back. The back of the neck should be at the back of the collar. The chest should be filled out, not caved in. In our system, we also stress eyes—use of eyes as an upper-body part.

The first and most important principle for the fourth part of the body—*the arms and hands*—is that there be an imaginary straight line from the elbow to the horse's mouth. If the horse is a little high-headed, follow his head, don't drop the hands to get his head down. The idea is to follow his head and push it down, not to pull it down. The second point is that the rider's thumbs are a couple of inches apart, and over and slightly in front of the withers. If the hands drop down, that imaginary straight line becomes a broken line below the mouth. If the hands are raised too high, there's a broken line above the mouth. In the correct position, the wrists, a prolongation of the forearm, follow the straight line and are not bent. The angle of wrists and thumbs is off the vertical about thirty degrees.

For mounting the whip should be in the left hand, not in the right hand. There's a very good reason for this. If the rider carries the whip in the right hand and in mounting manages to touch the horse's croup, there could be a very unpleasant accident. After mounting, the whip should be carried in either hand comfortably about three quarters toward the end over or in front of the rider's knee.

54. *A classic upper body—eyes up and trunk vertical at standstill.* One can only say that this is elegance in repose.

55. *A stiff upper body—shoulders pulled up.* Relax the shoulders and lift the chest and the head for an elegant posture.

56. *A sloppy upper body—roach-backed.* Not only does this posture look unattractive, but it also limits the rider's ability to use his back effectively to drive or to restrain.

57. *An artificial upper body—a hollow back.* "Posing" on a horse is self-centered and has nothing to do with riding a horse. Note the rigid back and lack of contact with the horse's mouth.

58. *Basic position of hands and arms—straight line from mouth to elbow*. As a rule, the most elastic relationship between rider's hand and horse's mouth is produced by this straight line.

59. *Hands and arms—a broken line below the mouth*. This hand position works on the bars of a horse's mouth. It is most useful in camouflaging or finessing a high head carriage on a hunter.

60. *Hands and arms—a broken line above the mouth.* This is a most useful position on a horse that lugs or roots down on the bit. However, it spoils the picture on a hunter or in an equitation class.

61. *Carrying a stick correctly.* Carry a stick or whip close to the end and let it rest either on your thigh or in front of your knee. Resting it toward your hip bone will twist your wrist.

Exercises

We now give beginners two exercises: our two-point and our three-point contact. These are very important exercises for developing position and habit. Two-point contact means that the seat is out of the saddle and just the two legs are in contact with the horse. With the seat back in the saddle, you have three-point contact. Sitting a trot is an exercise in three-point contact.

Have the rider shift the reins to the outside left hand. With the other hand reach up and grab the mane, and get up out of the saddle in two-point contact. This exercise does a number

62. *Two-point contact.* Only the rider's two legs are in contact with his horse. His seat is virtually out of the saddle.

63. *Three-point contact.* Now the rider's seat and two legs are in contact with his horse; thus three points of contact.

64. *Bridging the reins.* When riding with one hand, one crosses the free rein over the held rein and down through the palm of the hand. For a clearer demonstration I've left the bight of the rein (the loop) on this side of the photo. By rights the bight should be on the same side as the hand carrying the reins.

of things: It distributes weight into the heels from the seat and buttocks, and it also teaches the rider to get up off the horse's back when galloping and jumping. You want the rider to be up off the saddle about six inches.

Then have the rider go back into the saddle and drop the right arm in back of the right thigh. This gives a seat, a seat-bone seat.

I've mentioned that in my method we stress eyes, so let's discuss *looking as opposed to seeing.* If I look at a specific focal point, I still see everything around it. I see the bleachers, I see the people, I see the door, I see the ground, I see the rail. That is seeing as opposed to looking at a point. My seeing is my peripheral vision, and we keep on seeing. We teach looking as opposed to seeing to our riders, and we teach riding by looking and riding by seeing. In taking a jump, I see

65. *Eyes—looking at a point, the instructor.* The instructor, being a magnetic subject, is the most natural focal point for the student to concentrate on.

my distance. As I see my distance, I want to make a tight turn right as I'm taking off for my jump or on top of my jump. I *look* at my next jump. Riders at any level must understand the difference between looking as opposed to seeing.

So I give my students exercises to develop their eyes. The first one is riding in. This is the sequence: When I say, "Ride in," they look in at me, then they wait, then they turn and ride in. First they look at a point (the instructor), count one-two-three while waiting, and then ride in on the count of three and stop. Working at a slow sitting trot, we develop a habit that should hold when coming into a jump. You don't look at your jump and turn. You look at your jump, and then over there you turn, and then you jump. If you eliminate any of the three steps or do them out of order, it's wrong and creates hurried riding.

In the second exercise, I ask, "How do you turn a horse?" and they tell me: "Look, wait, and turn." Then they practice looking, waiting, and turning through two corners and a circle, concentrating on their eyes and exaggerating as they practice.

The third exercise is to establish a habit of riding under their eyes. They back the horses a step while looking at me; they cluck while looking at me; they tap with a stick while looking at me. What I am teaching my riders to do is to ride by "feel," not by "look." If you're going into a double combination at five feet, six inches and you look back at the first one as you're hitting the horse with a stick, what's going to happen at the second one? Maybe everything! The horse might run out; he might stop; he might sit in it. So the habits that we're introducing at this basic first-grade level are that whatever we do while riding a horse, we feel. We adjust a leg by feel. We use a stick by feel. We use a spur by feel. We use

66. *Eyes—looking at a point, a tree.* An inanimate object can now substitute for the instructor as a focal point.

67. *Eyes—"riding in."* The term "ride in" brings the individual or group in to the instructor for further explanation. This is another useful eye exercise.

68. *Eyes—riding a turn.* The first, last, and most important factor of riding a turn on a horse is the rider's eyes.

69. *Eyes—backing a horse.* Backing, as in any other schooling movement, should be done on a line; look up at a point.

70. *Eyes—incorrect; looking down at leg position and hands.* Looking down not only jeopardizes balance, but also greatly diminishes the automatic use of aids.

a leg by feel. We use hands by feel. We don't do these things by looking. However, teachers shouldn't underestimate the value of teaching eyes, training eyes, developing eyes. The single most important factor coming into a jump is eyes. You could have everything else wrong, but if you have your eyes trained and working, you have something going for you.

Upper-body Angulation at Gaits

The next topic is upper-body angulation at gaits. The upper-body angulation is controlled by the hip angle. We teach riding by considering four angles. The first is the ankle angle, the angle created by the foot and the shin. The second is the knee angle, the angle created by the rider's thigh and

71. *The four major angles.* We teach riding by controlling angles of the rider's body—namely, the ankle angle, the knee angle, the hip angle, and the elbow angle.

the top of his calf. The third is the hip angle, and that is the angle created by the thigh and the upper body. The fourth angle is the elbow angle.

At a standstill, the upper body is on the vertical to the ground. In backing, the upper body is still vertical. At a walk in hunter-seat equitation, the upper body is ever so slightly in front of the vertical, a tilt with the motion of the horse's walk. A rider too far back with his upper body is stiff. Often with a young rider if you stress too much dressage, you get a stiff, rigid upper body. If the upper body is tilted too far forward, you've got a perching rider, a passive rider.

In the slow sitting trot and the canter, the angulation is close to the vertical, but very slightly in front of it. In the posting trot, the hip angle closes so the upper-body angulation is approximately thirty degrees in front of the vertical.

72. *Rider's upper body—vertical at a standstill and for backing a horse.* The rider's hip angle is open and the upper body rests on a vertical line to the ground.

73. *Rider's upper body—slightly in front of vertical at walk, sitting trot, and canter.* The rider's hip angle is closed a couple of degrees and the upper body shifts ever so slightly in front of the vertical.

74. *Rider's upper body—inclined forward for posting, galloping, and jumping.* The rider's hip angle closes approximately thirty degrees in front of the vertical. Posting, galloping, and jumping with the motion of the horse are thus possible.

75. *Behind the motion at a posting trot.* The rider stays on the vertical and posts up and down rather than forward and up. This is useful for driving a horse into extension.

76. *Ahead of the motion at a posting trot.* The rider is in front of the vertical more than thirty degrees; the seat and crotch become very light. This position, due to its lack of drive, works well on a "cold" backed, sensitive, or hot horse.

This is posting with the motion of the horse. It is hunter-jumping riding, not dressage-test riding. They are different disciplines and should be treated as such—don't confuse the two.

So with the motion at sitting gaits the angulation is ever so slightly in front of the vertical, and in posting, galloping, and jumping, it's about thirty degrees in front of the vertical.

Exercises in Motion

Let's go now to riding without stirrups, and without taking the stirrups off the saddle. The rider takes his foot out of the stirrup and brings the buckle down about eighteen inches.

Then he crosses the stirrup over the wither so that the buckle is over the wither and upside down. The buckle should be upside down so that the stirrup is as flat as possible under the flap. If the buckle isn't turned over, the stirrup is bulky and it isn't conducive to sitting up in the front of the saddle. Then he does the same with the opposite stirrup. This is an example of how my approach to teaching is concerned with detail. Everything is detailed and broken down and broken down and broken down. I try to find a way to break it down farther, and better, as I go along.

Here are some exercises without stirrups that can readily be done as a group. Incidentally, one reason I prefer group work to private work as a rule is the competitive factor and the togetherness factor—watching another rider ride a line will help a rider ride a line, for example.

With the riders going to the right, have reins and sticks shifted to the left outside hand. Also shift the bight of the reins to the outside. The first exercise is to grab the pommel of the saddle with two fingers so that the rider can adjust his seat up into the pommel. As we do the other exercises, we come back to this position. And by holding the reins in the outside hand, there's a little more control and it keeps the rider's shoulders parallel to the horse, whereas if reins are in the inside hand, they'll be cutting in all the time and it'll twist the shoulders ahead of the horse's shoulders. So this is a preferable position. It's the adjustment position.

Now have them go to a slow sitting trot—about a six-mile-an-hour sitting trot. For the next exercise, I like dropping the right hand in back of the right thigh. Let it dangle and let them sit independently without holding the saddle; they should be stretching the lower leg back and down. Stretch it back and down in back of the girth a little bit.

77. *Correctly crossed stirrups.* The stirrup buckle must be pulled down from the bar at least eighteen inches, crossed over the withers upside down, and the leather placed flat under the flap. Otherwise the rider's thigh will be rubbed.

78. *Exercise without stirrups—holding the pommel.* The reins are held in the outside hand for better steering and the pommel is grasped by the inside hand in order to pull the seat, forklike, forward and down into the saddle.

79. *Exercise without stirrups—dangling the free arm.* This is the simplest exercise to do when one has let go of the saddle with his free hand.

80. *Exercise without stirrups—hand on hip.* Plant the free hand with the thumb behind the hip bone.

81. *Exercise without stirrups—rotation of arm.* Rotate the free arm, keeping it straight, forward, down, back, and up, and then reverse the rotation.

82. *Exercise without stirrups—twisting the trunk.* Hold the free arm still and parallel to the ground while twisting the trunk to the right and to the left. Looking back at the horse's tail with each rotation will insure that the exercise is fully accomplished.

Then, for other exercises, place the right hand on the right hip. Rotate the right arm in a circular motion, up and back, and down and up. Then reverse the rotation. Twist the trunk. Look back at the horse's tail. Hold the right arm up and keep it steady while looking back at the tail. Touch the horse's right ear. Have the rider touch his right toe, then his left toe, right toe, left toe. Touch the tail.

As teachers you can use these exercises plus your imagination. Isolate different parts of your rider's body—have him rotate his shoulder without letting his trunk rotate, or rotate his head without letting his trunk rotate, or rotate the foot. This isn't really to supple a rider as you would a dancer. What this sort of exercise does is isolate different parts of the body so that while one is in use another is steady and independent.

83. *Exercise without stirrups—touch horse's ear.* This is a wonderful exercise to strengthen legs, thighs, and seat for galloping and jumping work.

84. *Exercise without stirrups—touch toes.* Another wonderful exercise to make our rider tight. Be sure to reach down and actually touch the toes.

85. *Exercise without stirrups—touch horse's tail.* Reach back, look back, and actually touch the dock of the tail.

86. *Exercise without stirrups—rotating the head.* While keeping all other parts of the body steady and still practicing a head roll.

87. *Exercise without stirrups—rotating the foot.* This exercise produces flexibility of the ankle and foot. Keep the leg steady and in position while rotating the foot.

88. *Exercise without stirrups—knees in front of saddle.* Without the aid of gripping with the legs, one is forced to sit in the saddle and follow the movement of the horse in a natural and relaxed fashion.

Aids

It's time now to teach the rider about communication with the horse, about aids. The first thing we teach riders about aids is to separate natural vs. artificial aids. The back-up is a good teaching situation. It can be done with just hands, or legs and hands, natural aids. It can be done with a cluck and hands and legs, natural aids. So we teach what the natural aids are: legs, weight, hands, and voice. Then we show it done with a spur, an artificial aid. Or with a stick, also an artificial aid, as are bits and martingales and auxiliary reins.

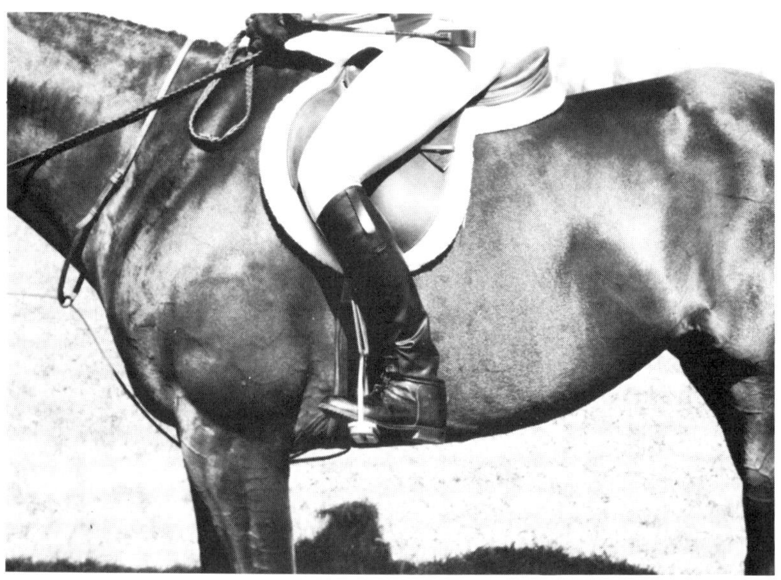

89. *Hands as an aid (closing).* To use the hands, one closes on the reins as if squeezing a lemon. In basic, slow work it is wrong to pull back on the reins,

90. *Legs as an aid* (*squeezing*). To use the legs one squeezes lightly. Any more work than that, such as kicking, is out of the question. We then resort to a stick, a spur, or a cluck.

91. *Weight as an aid (driving or restraining)*. By stretching the spine up and back we are in a strong position either to drive forward or to hold back.

I don't let beginners use spurs. Legs are not spurs, spurs are not legs. They are separate aids. One is natural; one is artificial. One is advanced; one is basic and simple. A rider shouldn't have a spur until he's a decent intermediate, maybe even a top intermediate. A beginner should never have a spur because he has no leg control yet. His leg slips all over, slides all over. If his horse bucks, the beginner has no independence of leg and he's going to hit the horse with his spur, and the horse is going to buck harder. Or if his horse bolts and runs away and the rider has a spur, he's going to grip with his leg and he's going to compound the runaway with his spur. So

92. *Voice as an aid (cluck or "whoa").* To cluck correctly use the side of the mouth, the tongue, and the roof of the mouth; not the front of the mouth and lips in a kissing action. The use of "whoa" should be soft and low, not loud and harsh, which would only frighten the horse into going faster.

don't think of a spur and a leg as the same. They're not even in the same category. As I've said, one is artificial; one is natural. Moreover, you don't ride every horse with a spur. You select the horse that you're riding with a spur. You can ride some horses over fences without a spur. It is a very selective, important choice when I'm showing horses, as to which ones I ride with a spur and which I don't ride with a spur.

A very important lesson we teach about aids concerns

clashing of aids. A beginner is going to walk his horse forward and he's going to pull him a little. And he's going to stop his horse and grip him a little with his legs. That's basic clashing of aids, wherein the rider is working against his legs with his hands or vice versa. Now suppose the rider asks the horse to jump, and the rider gets left back. He's clashing his aids. Or he hits the horse with a stick back of the saddle while pulling the reins. That's another example of clashing the aids. This is why I don't teach people to put their horses on the bit with flexion at this level of riding. Beginners aren't up to coordinating their aids to get flexion.

93. *Spurs as an aid.* The spur should be parallel to the heel seam of the boot and not necessarily over the spur rest. For basic work I prefer Prince of Wales spurs.

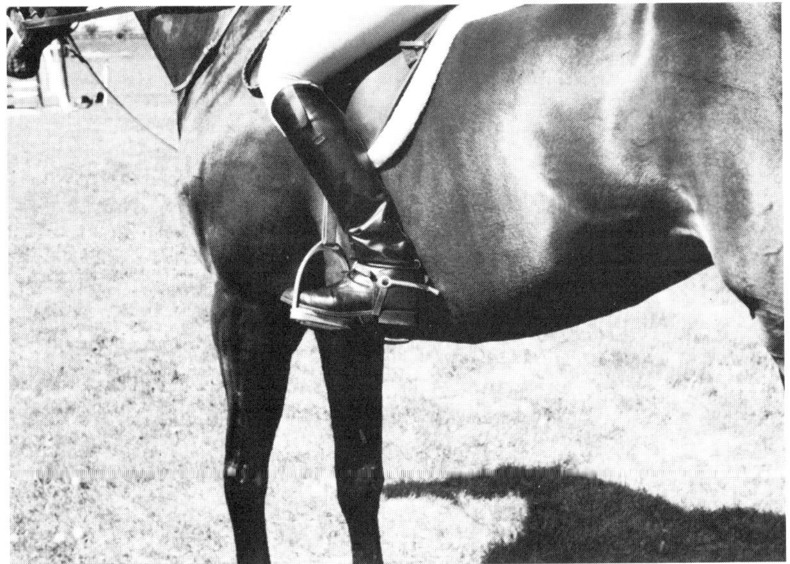

94. *Stick as an aid.* To use the stick correctly: One bridges the reins, strokes back of the saddle with the stick, comes back to the reins in both hands. It should take no more than half a second.

95. *Clashing of aids—pushing and pulling.* This is a cardinal sin, asking the horse to go forward and come back at the same time. Notice the horse pinning her ears and swishing her tail.

There are two stages to getting a horse *on the bit*. In the colt stage, the young-horse stage, he takes the bit like a straight stick and pulls a little. In the second stage, the rider keeps engaging and urging the horse until he compresses and gets in a rounded frame and demonstrates flexion as he's pulling a little. Beginners can't possibly co-ordinate (they don't even understand where flexion comes from) the hind leg of the horse. Nor is an intermediate rider able to produce the correct flexion in a horse. Wait until you get to advanced riding, by which I mean good tenth-grade riding, medal riding. A good junior should be taught how to produce flexion, but if you teach that too early, you'll cause clashing of aids, which is a major sin on a horse.

So we teach what clashing is, and then we teach *co-ordination of aids*. Have the students walk their horses. Have them stop their horses by closing on the horse's mouth and relaxing their legs—not taking away the position of their legs or taking a leg off the horse, just making their legs passive as they activate their hands. Now have them relax their hands and ask their horses to walk by squeezing and closing their legs. That's a basic example of co-ordination.

Now have students back up by squeezing legs and hands. As long as we teach it in a back-up, it's co-ordination. If students ask their horses to stop that way, that's clashing. If they want their horses to walk that way, that's clashing. If they want them to back up, that's co-ordination. So establish the idea of clashing as opposed to co-ordinating very early with your riders.

We also now teach them about their *outside aids vs. their inside aids*. We keep it simple at this stage. We teach them that their outside rein is opposite the instructor; their inside rein is close to their instructor or the center of the ring. This

96. *On the bit—first stage.* The rider has a soft, steady contact with the horse's mouth. The horse is likewise taking the hand with a soft and steady pull. There is not necessarily any flexion or yield from the jaw or poll at this stage.

97. *On the bit—second stage.* All the factors of the first stage still hold true, with the exception that now the horse has yielded (flexed) his jaw, his poll, and his hocks. Note that the horse's face is just in front of the vertical, and his neck is stretched and low.

98. *Above the bit.* This is a very common sight. The horse's hocks are out to the rear, stiff and unyielding; his back is dropped and hollow; and his head and neck are up and out with no flexion at the jaw or poll.

99. *Behind the bit.* The worst evasion to the bit's action, perhaps, is when the horse tucks his chin in and completely refuses to take hold of the bit. Notice how the contact of the reins is slack, the horse's face almost behind the vertical, and the highest point is the middle of the neck rather than the poll.

100. *Outside vs. inside aids on a turn.* The outside rein predominates and regulates the track and the impulsion; the inside rein supports and controls the bend. The inside leg predominates in creating impulsion and controlling straightness, while the outside leg supports both the impulsion and the straightness.

doesn't always hold true, of course. Later, when we're working with an intermediate, we confuse him. For example, if he's going to the right and he's working a left shoulder-in—well, his outside rein is near the instructor, and his inside rein is opposite the instructor. But that would bewilder a beginner. A beginner is not ready to know that. He shouldn't know that. It should be kept very much a beginner's conception that the outside aids are away from the center of the ring, and the inside aids are toward the instructor and the center. Keep it simple. But with the future in mind, it's better to say, "Affect your horse with your outside rein" than "with your left hand," or "push him from your inside leg," not "push him from your right leg."

It's time now to teach *lateral vs. diagonal aids.* We show that lateral aids are on the same side. For instance, bend the horse with the right rein and the right leg. A beginner's hands should be over and in front of the wither. An exercise in diagonal aids is to bend the horse with the right indirect rein while at a standstill, and to move his haunch to the right with the left leg. The very beginning level of rider isn't up to doing much with diagonal aids, only with lateral ones, but they can be taught the terminology.

Now you want your beginners to go into a canter using outside lateral aids. Going to the right, it's left rein, left leg. Going to the left, it's right rein, right leg.

101. *Diagonal aids for the canter depart.* The horse is slightly bent in the direction of movement with the inside rein and leg; his haunches are displaced in the direction of movement with the outside leg. Because the opposite rein and leg predominate, we have diagonal aids.

What about the *cluck* as an aid? First, we teach the cluck as an aid like a leg or a driving aid. Second, we teach a beginner how to teach his horse to respond to a cluck. Take a green horse out of a field and he probably won't respond to a cluck. He'll listen to a cluck and prick his ears, but he won't go forward. So we teach the horse to associate a cluck and a little stick. Then a cluck is associated with a leg by squeezing the horse and giving a little cluck. Always associate a cluck with a stronger driving aid like a leg or a stick so that the horse is constantly conditioned to respond to the cluck. The cluck isn't important; the stick isn't important; the leg isn't important. It's the response that is important. Teach your beginners the response to the aid through this exercise with the cluck and the stick.

As for the *stick,* we don't let beginners use a stick by holding the rein in the same hand. We teach them in a sequence. Shift the rein to the other hand. Step one: Reach back, tap the horse, and come back to the reins. Separate the reins. That's the little exercise.

I teach an advanced rider to tap the horse on the neck while holding the rein, because he won't clash his aids. But lower intermediates or beginners will jerk their horses. As for reaching back of the saddle and holding onto the reins, that's the worst clash. So we teach them step one: Bridge the reins. Step two: Reach back of the saddle. Step three: Go right back to the reins. And they're going to do it in a count of three: one, two, three. Then in a count of two: one, two. Then in a count of one as one movement. That's proper teaching. The wrong way is to yell, "Hit him with a stick! Hit him with a stick!" The idea is to have a teaching approach that is specific and practical and detailed enough. Too much teaching of riding isn't broken down; steps aren't analyzed or

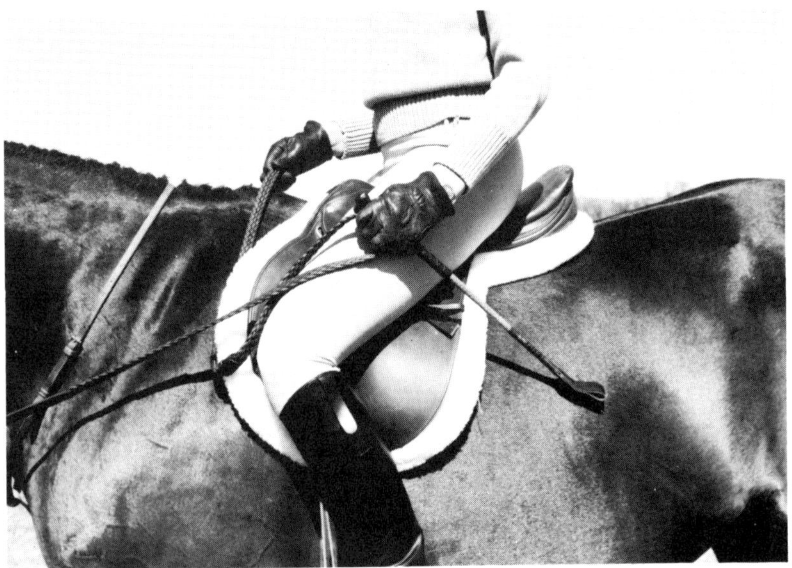

102. *Incorrect use of the stick.* While holding the rein and hitting the horse in the mouth, this short stick is being applied back of the saddle. This is a cardinal sin and an extreme clashing of aids.

103. *Incorrect use of the stick.* By hitting a horse on the shoulder in this fashion, we do not produce sufficient forward response and are apt to hit our horse in the mouth by mistake. I do allow advanced riders this tap on the shoulder at a jump just as a minor reinforcement to legs.

taught in sequences as in the methods of teaching physics or Latin or in some other sports today.

There are two positions for the *leg* as an aid. You have the position at the back edge of the girth—that's the position for driving a horse forward, and that's the position for bending him the length of his body. That's position one. The second basic position to use the leg as an aid is back of the girth by a hand's length. Now, when I teach a position, I teach a function. I don't ever teach a position without a function. I'm trying to give you the trick for making riders both attractive and able. The trick to that is, first, position, and right on top of it, function.

Many teachers produce beautiful positions in their riders, but their riders can't ride. Then there are teachers who develop riders who are aggressive and effective, but they evidence no finesse or sophistication or polish or appeal on a hunter. I don't want either appeal or ability; I want both. I would want all my riders to be like Billy Steinkraus at their level of conformation and talent and temperament. I want them to use their positions as attractively as possible, and I want them to go in and give anybody a run for his money in the Grand Prix if they're up to that. That's what I'm trying to teach riding teachers to strive for.

Now, with the second position of leg, back a hand, the rider can displace the haunch a little bit. That can be taught at a standstill. Put the leg back and squeeze; the haunch moves away from the pressure. Then we'll use that to go into a canter.

After the two basic positions for leg aids, there are the five basic positions for *rein aids*. The first is a direct rein aid. This is from front to back, a direct rein. The rider can back the horse with a direct rein, front to back. The second rein aid is

104. *Direct rein.* A direct rein is a straight line from the rider's elbow to the horse's mouth; it controls the horse from front to rear.

an indirect rein, in opposition to the horse's haunch—an indirect rein over in front of the horse's withers toward the rider's outside hip.

There's another indirect rein aid that we don't teach at this stage but that an instructor might keep in mind. It, too, is in the direction of the horse's opposite haunch, but it is a little back of the withers and in, not over and out as much.

Then there is the leading or opening rein aid. We teach this with corresponding exercises, such as "Go through the corner," or "Lead your horse through the corner." We give simple schooling movements right away after we've taught the position of the rein. For instance, we say, "Now bend your horse through the corner. Now stop your horse with a direct rein. Now go through a circle with an indirect rein. Now go through a serpentine with a leading or opening rein."

105. *Indirect rein in front of the withers.* This rein aid goes from the horse's mouth through the withers to the rider's opposite hip. It produces a bend in the horse's neck and displaces weight to the opposite shoulder.

106. *Indirect rein in rear of the withers.* An intermediary rein aid between the opening rein and the indirect rein in front of the withers, the line goes from the horse's mouth to the horse's opposite haunch. This rein aid bends the neck and displaces weight to that opposite haunch.

107. *Leading or opening rein.* This is the most basic, primitive way to steer a horse. The pressure is sideways, never backward; and we pull him softly in the desired direction.

108. *Neck or bearing rein.* The hands shift over in the desired direction. Again there is no backward pull. The pressure works against the shoulder.

We also have a pulley rein and a neck rein. The neck rein is used against the horse's shoulder to push him off that shoulder. That's a very useful rein aid. For the pulley rein, the rider sets the knuckles of his inside hand in the wither and comes up and back with the outside hand. That isn't a very good rein aid to use as a crutch, but it's a rough and quick rein, an emergency rein aid.

Weight isn't an independent aid; it's a helping aid. By itself it doesn't work, ever. It's impossible for weight to work by itself. When the rider stretches his back, it's got to help the reins or the legs. Weight is a natural aid, but only a reinforcement aid. There are two types of upper body or back for a rider. The first is a relaxed back. The second is a braced back. This is a stretch in which the rider pulls the chest up

109. *Pulley rein.* I always refer to this rein aid as an emergency brake. The knuckles or heel of the inside hand are set just in front of the withers, while the outside hand comes back on the horse's mouth. In turning, one sets the outside hand and turns with the inside hand.

110. *Weight as an aid to restrain or drive.* The rider's weight as an aid can never be used alone; it is helpless. However, when co-ordinated with legs to drive or hands to restrain, it becomes an overwhelmingly powerful force.

111. *On the correct diagonal.* Notice how the rider's seat is up out of the saddle as her horse's right foreleg is forward and up off the ground. She is said to be on the right (vs. the left) diagonal. This lightens not only the outside shoulder but also the inside haunch.

and back a little, not the shoulders, not leaning back. It's stretching up and back against the horse. We use this when we want to ask a horse to do something. Have the rider back the horse while stretching the spine. Then walk the horse while stretching. Turn the horse on his forehand a step while stretching the spine. That's weight as an aid. It's very, very simple. It is a reinforcement to leg or hand. It isn't ever used alone, as I've said. Either you ask a horse to go or you ask him to stop, or you ask him to turn, and you reinforce with your weight.

Diagonals and Leads

At this stage of riding, the rider is posting on, say, the outside diagonal by checking the outside shoulder. It isn't time yet to teach beginning riders to feel diagonals or leads. Don't teach them to look for diagonals or leads. Don't teach them

112. *Looking down—wrong.* Only in the earliest stages of learning diagonals and leads do I permit a rider to drop his head and eyes and look down.

to look over and lean down. Teach them to check by glancing down. At this level an instructor may allow a rider to drop his head and eyes. It's also permissible to check the lead going into a canter by looking at the horse's inside shoulder. When teaching riders diagonals and leads at this first stage, let them —in fact, encourage them—to look down with the head; not with the body, but just with the head and eyes.

I find that checking the outside shoulder is a little easier for diagonals and the inside shoulder for leads. But that's a point that could be either way—like the little finger inside or outside the rein. Either way could be right. If you've had success with the inside shoulder, keep the inside shoulder; just so your system is consistent. Let me stress: Whatever your system is of teaching a point or several points or an entire system of teaching, be consistent. Don't jump from one system to another. Don't have a mishmash of systems. Any system at all is better than no system at all. Don't say, "Well, today we're going to do the outside shoulder. Well, no, this one likes the inside shoulder. Let's have the inside shoulder. Well, I think I'm wrong. Now I think I'd better go back to the outside shoulder. Oh well, I really don't care which way you do it." That's very poor teaching.

All of my riders ride with their little finger outside the rein —because it's my system and I say it's right. So they'll all be all right. Another teacher says, "All of my riders ride with the little finger inside the rein because I know it's right." They'll be all right. But the teacher who says "inside" today, "outside" tomorrow, or "whichever you like, do," has no system. The same holds true for a parallel toe. I want the toe out a shade. But either way is all right, as long as you are definite about your system and stick with it. The teacher who's wishy-washy about his system won't ever be a good teacher no matter what he does.

113. *Glancing down—right*. Glancing down with eyes only prohibits a rider from dropping his head. It is a preferable way of checking diagonals and leads and is invisible to the onlooker too!

114. *Feel—don't look!* The experience of hours in the saddle gives us feel. Then and only then, by feel alone, can we check our diagonal or lead.

I've been criticized for teaching that beginners should grab the mane. I'm like the guy Up There: I give and then I take it away. We teach them to grab the mane, then we teach them not to grab the mane. We teach them to ride with a feel of the mouth over a jump, then we teach them not to ride with a feel of the mouth over a jump. We teach them to ride with a leg and we teach them to ride without a leg; with a spur, without a spur. An able teacher can teach riders to do the same thing in many different ways. So we'll teach them at this stage to look down at the diagonal or the lead. At the next stage we teach them to glance, not drop the head, just the eyes. But I expect my top riders to know by feel. I don't want them to drop the head or eyes. I want them just to feel. I've given a technique of looking down, then I take it away at a later time. In the same way, I give the technique of grabbing the mane, then I take it away.

Control

We teach two types of controls on a horse. The first type is longitudinal control. The second is lateral control. And we teach these very, very early along with teaching pace. Pace should be taught through miles per hour. If you ask riders how fast they're going at a walk, one will say, "two miles an hour"; another says, "six miles an hour"; and another says, "five miles an hour." Well, a walk is approximately four miles an hour. We teach basic pace control and understanding by teaching miles per hour.

It's helpful to know roughly how many miles per hour at a walk and also, of course, at a trot, a canter, and a gallop. So we teach pace rather than use terms such as "shorten stride,"

115. *Longitudinal control—backing*. This is a co-ordination of legs and hands. The hands close and prevent the horse from moving forward, while the legs actively move the horse backward.

"lengthen stride," "impulsion," and so on. A slow trot, a sitting trot, or, later, a collected trot is six miles an hour. A posting trot is eight miles an hour. A canter is approximately ten to twelve miles an hour. And a hand gallop is approximately fourteen to sixteen miles an hour. So the first thing we teach as a habit about pace control is learning to associate pace with miles per hour. Then we'll work on increases and decreases—simple ones like trotting and stopping, sitting trot, posting trot, sitting trot, and canter. We never let beginners post into a canter or run the horse into a canter. We ask them to go from a slow trot into a canter. Later on, at a higher level, they go from a walk into a canter. So the increases and decreases are longitudinal controls. What about a simple lead change? That's a *longitudinal control.*

I teach many things at a standstill on a horse because it's simpler for me; and the beginner doesn't have to worry about the horse going anywhere. I also teach backing early—simple elementary backing with just closing hands for a step or two. Then I teach backing by closing legs and hands. Next, backing with a cluck and closing legs and hands; then, backing with a stick and closing legs and hands. I get the aids working at a standstill, at a back-up, in slow motion, so when I get into jumping work, the aids are firmly planted in my students.

In teaching *lateral control,* we start with bending in the corners, and we teach the sequence of looking, then bending with hands, looking, then an indirect rein, and then an inside leg—the lateral controls. After working on corners, we go to circling. Circling is a great precision exercise. It means starting at a given point and finishing at that point. I'm not interested in the circle. I'm interested in developing precision. That's the great value of dressage. Also, if the instructor has a beginner on a fresh horse put him right on a circle, and as

116. *Bending.* A horse is properly bent when his head, neck, and body are all curved in equal proportion. If rounding a turn, the degree of bend should correspond to the degree of the turn.

117. *Lateral control—circling.* The circle is one of the first exercises to teach the horse to bend and to turn. Note the even bend of the horse from head to tail while his tracking remains straight.

that horse settles down, let him go out on the circle a little bigger and a little bigger. The circle will take the beginner's mind off worrying. Moving in a circle takes the horse's mind off *his* ideas, and yet gives him no place to go. In fact, I teach a beginner right off the bat about a runaway horse. When he's got a runaway on his hands, if he does nothing else, he must put the horse on a circle with one rein and keep him on a circle until eventually the horse stops.

118. *Imaginary jump—posting with the motion.* A rider does not actually need to jump to learn how to jump. Here we can see the first basic of jumping, control of the upper body in a forward position to be with the motion of the horse.

III
Teaching the Beginner to Jump

In my system, I start beginners jumping, theoretically, right when they start—they're hopping over little obstacles as soon as they learn to ride. We don't wait, first teaching them how to ride for a year or two, then teaching them how to jump the second or third year. The first thing I teach a rider about jumping is that when he's able to post a trot, he's able to jump an imaginary jump. Everything we do on the flat is geared toward jumping a fence. It's not a system that's devoted to test dressage but to jumping courses.

The Fundamentals

We teach *posting with the motion.* That means the rider's upper body is at an angle thirty degrees off the vertical. The horse's thrust is posting the rider; it is not the rider posting the rider but the horse posting the rider. So the first thing you teach somebody about taking a jump is posting a trot correctly with the motion.

The second thing we teach our rider about taking a jump is the use of his *eyes,* which means working with focal points and on a line and stopping on a line. The instructor can be

119. *Imaginary jump—eyes on a point.* Looking at and going to a point is riding a line, in practice straightness. This is the second fundamental of jumping, the rider's eyes.

the focal point. The rider should look at the instructor, then ride right up and stop directly in front of him. If the rider's approach is wrong, then the jump is going to be wrong. If the rider is off the focal point by ten feet—well, even one foot is just about as bad as ten feet. Now the rider posts over an imaginary jump with the motion and looking at a focal point and stops on a line.

As the third step, I teach the three phases of *working with a line*. The first is looking through the turns. The second is riding out on a line. And the third is stopping on a line. Also, I keep going back, reviewing and reminding riders to post with the motion. So far, we have the upper bodies working thirty degrees off the vertical. We've given the conception of the horse's thrust, his posting the rider. There's also thrust at

120. *Imaginary jump—riding and stopping on a line.* Here the instructor's right hand is the focal point at the end of the imaginary center line through the obstacle.

the jump, when the horse's thrust closes the rider forward and up for the jump. Riders should never duck and jump ahead of the horse. It's the horse's thrust that throws their bodies, not the other way around. That's why I keep reviewing the posting trot because a posting trot and a jump are identical—not close, *identical.* That's why we don't work riders at a sitting trot to a jump—not at this level of riding. Later on, at a more advanced level, we can work them at a sitting trot. Then we have them by habit using their eyes, looking and then riding and then stopping with their eyes on a specific point, a focal point, so they get in the habit of riding a line and working with a straight horse.

Step four for teaching beginners to jump an obstacle is *use of the hands.* We teach a release with the hands, and we call

121. *A long release grabbing mane—at a standstill.* Moving her hands halfway up the horse's crest, the rider grabs the mane. The long release puts the rider's upper body into the correct jumping position, inclined forward.

it a release, and we keep labeling it a release even when we go into different types of releases. The first release I teach is grabbing the mane, and we teach it at a standstill. The rider reaches halfway up the horse's crest and grabs the mane there. Be very sure it's halfway up—not too far and definitely not too short a release. And the beginner should reach for the mane two or three strides out in front of the jump. The sequence is to post with the motion, look at a focal point, reach up and grab the mane, and stop on a line.

As the fifth step we introduce two-point contact, which we've already taught as an exercise. The rider bridges the

122. *A long release grabbing mane—imaginary jump.* About three strides away from the jump the rider moves into the long release and, thus, insures a correct upper-body position. Horses that refuse or run out with this release shouldn't be ridden by beginners.

123. *Two-point contact for legs and heels—imaginary jump.* Bridging the reins in the outside hand and grabbing the mane halfway up the crest with the inside hand help the rider hold a two-point contact. This particular exercise encourages the weight to be displaced from seat to heels.

reins in the outside hand, reaches up and catches the mane halfway up the crest, and gets up out of the saddle about six inches. The concentration now goes into the rider's legs and heels. The crotch shouldn't have to be too far out of the saddle, but the seat and buttocks should be up out of the saddle at least six inches, so that the weight is definitely out of the saddle and into the heels.

You can also use this sort of imaginary jumping with an adult who's had a fall and never wants to jump again. You can say, "Well, we're going to do some jumping with you just as a suppling exercise, just to give you a little suppling work." People like the word "suppling." It distracts them, and no horseman or rider will ever argue that he shouldn't have suppling work or that a horse shouldn't have suppling work. Then you go on to another kind of jump for them and for beginners.

Cavalletti and Crossrails

I use a low-jump system to teach. I don't want the rider's concentration on the jump. I want the concentration on the technique—on release, for instance, not "Oh it's a three-foot jump!" A three-foot jump to an intermediate and to a beginner is a very big jump. Crossrails, cavalletti, low jumps—these jumps are anything up to two feet, six inches. Beyond that, two feet, six inches to three feet, six inches or three feet, nine inches, are medium jumps. Anything over three feet, nine inches is a big jump for the average rider. This clinic is a teachers' clinic for the average beginner, so it's just cavalletti and crossrails. In my opinion Bert de Nemethy's program is also built largely on the low-jump system.

When I was with Gordon Wright, we used to call the very first sort of beginner's jump a rail on the ground. Now it's called "cavalletti." Great mystery and importance are attached to cavalletti. Whole careers have been built on cavalletti and books written about nothing but cavalletti. Well, they're no mystery. And they're all right. A cavalletti's a stabilizer. I'm told that just one should be called a cavalletto, but that's getting too fancy, so I generally call them cavalletti whether it's one or more. It does muscle horses' backs to some degree, but it's not the end-all and the be-all. It is another exercise, like standing in the stirrups or a shoulder-in or an oxer or a vertical or a stop or a back-up. It's no bet-

124. *Cavalletti in rhythm—four to five feet apart.* Cavalletti work stabilizes a horse's pace and instills a sense of rhythm in the rider. It also promotes the horse's attention and use of himself.

125. *Eyes down—wrong.* Looking down causes a loss of balance and interferes with the use of the aids. Eyes are so important; they are responsible for directional movement and timing.

ter and no worse than that. Don't overromanticize use of cavalletti. It's a stabilizer. It's a very good exercise, but don't think that it's the salvation to any problem on any horse. People go over and over cavalletti until they're blue in the face—six, eight, ten of them in a row; and they think they're going to muscle up the horse and they think cavalletti is going to make every one of them jump like a horse that won a gold medal. They think the cavalletti is going to do all kinds of magic for them. That's hogwash. I like cavalletti in their place. I like them as I like riding crops. In their place.

At first, don't ask beginners to do "spacing"—that is, three or four, cavalletti; just a single rail on the ground, one cavalletti. The difference between one rail and an imaginary jump is entirely psychological. There's no thrust yet. There's just the horse stepping over. Possibly the horse will hop over it and provide a thrill.

Next we're definitely going to give the rider a thrill because we're going to use a crossrail, and the horse has to hop over. Most horses will hop over it. Very few horses will step over it. It should be about a six-inch crossrail jump. The instructor should remember repetition. The riders post with the motion, use their eyes, concentrate on their release, two-point contact, and they've got their little thrill. The purpose of this step-by-step system—first no jump, then a rail on the ground, then a crossrail jump, and then a straight rail jump—is to establish habit.

So this is the lesson in teaching. If you're sloppy about one part of the body, then you're going to have trouble with another part of the body. If you don't make sure that beginners follow through with their arms and hands, you're going to develop riders who jump out ahead of a horse at a jump or who fall back. Most instructors when teaching jumping will

126. *A short crest release at a standstill.* A short release will become an automatic reaction, providing a long release has been taught first. This release moves up the crest only a few inches, the hands pressing down and in. The weight of the upper body is partly supported by the hands.

127. *Heels up over cavalletti—wrong.* Not only does this faulty leg position jeopardize the rider's security, but it also irritates the horse. The rider's heels and ankles are his shock absorbers.

have their riders too far behind—a result of violating basics. If the heels pop up, there will be a loose leg and the rider will drop back. And a six-inch jump to a rider at this level is a big step psychologically and physically, so we attack that step and solve it before we even move on to using the crossrail.

Co-ordinating Exercises

Now we're going to start associating basic co-ordinations at a jump. The first step is "brake" and then "gas." With a beginner, I release the brake and then I add gas. With an intermediate or advanced rider I add the gas, push him up into the brake, then I release the brake. For an intermediate it's the

128. *An in-and-out—holding two-point contact.* The rider's seat and crotch stay out of the saddle for the duration of the two jumps. This is more of an exercise to combat dropping back.

reverse of the procedure for a beginner. The beginner is to release—reach up and catch the mane—about thirty feet out from the jump and then squeeze the horse over. We do that exercise about ten times to develop a habit of co-ordination—first release the brake, then add gas.

Then we give them a second exercise. Reach up, then cluck (one cluck) to get the horse over. About here we might graduate to a crossrail and then a sequence of obstacles and maybe on to a straight rail after the crossrail.

And we add another exercise. We have them concentrate on this sequence: First they post with the motion to the first jump; they look up and over the two jumps; and they concentrate on their hands. They have two types of hands. First is the feel; second is the release, which is halfway up the crest, where a beginner grabs the mane. They concentrate on this

129. *An in-and-out—dropping back and sitting down—wrong.* Dropping back or coming back into the saddle during the flight of the jump is wrong.

130. *An in-and-out sinking into crotch-three-point contact.* Here the rider softly sinks into her saddle to support the horse for the next fence—in other words, she is using her weight as an aid.

sequence of feel, release, feel, release, feel, stop. When beginners have two jumps in a row and maybe a slightly bigger jump as the second one, they may be a little apprehensive. I use this sequence as a distraction principle when there's mental and physical fear. Feel, release, feel, release, feel, stop—that's hard for a beginner. They're so cluttered mentally that they don't have time to be worried psychologically about the two jumps and the bigger jump, and I don't care what they do as long as they do feel, release, feel, release, feel, stop.

Next we have them concentrate on cantering a jump. They post the first jump, just as they did before, using the exercises of distraction, and go into a canter for the second jump. These are specific and acute progressions for a beginner. First they do two jumps. Then the second is a bigger jump—say, two feet. And third, they work at a canter. What I use is a gymnastic principle. The entrance is easy; the exit is difficult. They've done the entrance over and over just as a single obstacle. The exit is difficult but they don't know it's difficult or think it's difficult. It's the same thing you do when you want to teach a young green jumper scope and give him confidence. You keep the cavalletti rail, then have a little vertical, then make the oxer bigger and bigger and wider and wider, and even though the horse may only have jumped five or six times in his life, he might end up going over a very big oxer. The exit is very difficult, but it's presented by the entrance so simply that the horse doesn't know it's difficult. Well, that's exactly the same principle that we use with beginning riders.

Also I believe strongly in forming the habit of riding a turn, riding a line, and stopping on a line. It must be absolutely precise, and you should give a beginner a principle of riding and schooling a horse whereby he doesn't go to the

131. *Use of stick at take-off.* After having practiced this technique at a standstill and in motion, the rider must learn to co-ordinate the stick with the horse's motion.

next thing until he's finished the job he's working on. An instructor should make them practice going through a corner, taking two jumps on the line, and stopping at an exact point on that line.

When they're ready, we graduate to an in-and-out of crossrails, and we let our beginners canter now. A beginner must be releasing the horse at a beginner level of release, which means releasing him thoroughly, letting him be a loose horse. A stick may be used, but only at a standstill to encourage more animation or as punishment for a refusal. An instructor should keep the horses carrying beginners over their jumps, little jumps, with a cluck at the take-off. Beginners shouldn't try to use a stick at a take-off because they're not ready for that. If there's no stick and the horse is hesitant and sluggish and has to be put up to the bit, beginners should be taught to use a slap with the hand as a stick, clucking at the same time.

Summary

This is essentially the end of the work, as far as points and exercises are concerned, that I would want to do with beginners, because anything farther than this carries the rider into the intermediate category. At this stage, the beginner should have his upper body working automatically at the posting trot and slow gallop. He should be looking up and over his jumps, not looking for a distance. He should be looking up and over his jumps at a point. He should be working on a line and he should be riding out his line and he should be stopping on a line as a habit. About two or three strides in front of a jump he should be automatically reaching up and grabbing mane halfway up the crest. He should have the weight in his heels, not in his buttocks or his knees. He should be able to work in two-point contact as an exercise or hold it as he's going through an in-and-out.

He should have had imaginary jumps. He should have had work over cavalletti. He should have had crossrails and straight rails. He should be based in simple co-ordination—releasing his brake and applying gas, which is leg. He should do a simple sequence of obstacles such as two jumps in a row, or three on a spaced-out row, or a simple in-and-out. He should post a jump or he should canter a simple jump. He shouldn't jump yet at a sitting trot. He should have his upper body under control so that he approaches an in-and-out with

132. *Jumping incorrectly—the "grip" is wrong.* The rider is gripping with her knees and thighs. There is no distribution of contact into the lower leg.

133. *Ducking—wrong.* Here the rider is throwing herself at her horse instead of allowing the horse's thrust to close her upper body forward and upward. Ducking is not only rough and unattractive but also will make a quick horse quicker.

134. *Jumping ahead—wrong.* Notice how the rider's seat and crotch are almost in front of the pommel. This is the most serious of faults involving the base and upper body. If the horse should stop, the rider could dismount in a hurry!

135. *Correct upper body in the air.* The horse is doing the jumping, not the rider. There should be no excess of motion in the rider's upper body.

the motion. As he goes through an in-and-out, he's up ahead of the motion. After he's done the in-and-out, he's with the motion. As a beginner, he shouldn't ever be asked to ride behind the motion, which means on the buttocks, in the upright, or on the vertical position.

Riders at this stage should keep with the motion or ahead of the motion, never behind the motion, which results in getting left back at a jump. The beginner at this stage should be able to co-ordinate releasing his brake and a cluck as well as his leg as gas. He should be versed in use of the stick, but only at a standstill in front of the jump to create animation and educate the horse for a strange jump or to punish for a refusal. He should know how to punish a refusal with a stick. He should know how to cope with a refusal. He should be aware that a slap is a stick if he's caught without a stick. If he's going cross-country without a stick and his horse stops, it should be an automatic reaction to slap his horse if necessary. He should be able to sit a slow trot, really a jog trot. He should be able to recognize the correct diagonal and lead, and he should be able to use the direct and indirect rein properly.

I hope that, over-all, what I've been able to teach you about teaching is, first, give the rider the positive, then take away the negative. Don't take away the negative and then give the positive. For instance, if a rider has a roached back, it's because he's dropping his head and chin. Give the exercise of touching the neck to the back of the collar, of keeping eyes up. That should correct the back. If a rider is ducking over a jump, reinforce the two-point contact position rather than saying, "Don't duck." Give the positive tools first; then you eliminate the negatives. And always remember that the basics in beginner work are the essential foundations for intermediate and advanced riding.

136. *Concentration.* Always think about what's ahead; never look back!

The slow way of teaching is the quick way to learn to ride; and the quick way of teaching insures slow progress. Rome was not built in a day, nor are safe, educated, and versatile horsemen developed in a day. Good luck and just remember to go slow and low.

DEC 50 50 £100
JAN 50 50 £100
FEB 50 50 £100
£100
MARCH 50 50 £100
APRIL 50 50 £1000
MAY 50 50

M	K	F	UP	
£20	£20	£30	£60	£120 MONTH

£190 MONTH